When They Were

Were

MattDrudge DianeSa
zKafkaF.ScottFitzgerald Mr.
kyDr.Seuss RobertRedford
odyGuthrieStanleyKubrick Curtis
eyHepburn DavidHasselhoff
mani Estée Lauder
StephenH RichardBransonSe
unterS.Thompson
DianeSawyerSh
coChanelJerryGarci
RobertCrumb
amieFoxxNorahJonesS
DavidBowieJerry
GarnerJanisJoplin
nJ.EdgarHoover
yCash DorothyParker
JohnBelushiPamelaAnderson
velaceRaymondCarverRobertAltman
SeanConnery JerryFalwell
dy"CombsRingoStarrErnestHeming
LewinskyBradPittAnselAdams

OprahWinfreyCheech
RalphNader MalcolmXEliot
BillMurraySusanSarandon
onsSandraDayO'Connor GarthBrook
oseanneBarr FrankZappa RodSerli
J.D.Salinger RonaldReagan
riciaCornwellJim HelenKelle
SissySpacek
ChristieBrinkleyZa
ronStoneHowardSt
SteveMartin
AliceWalkerDesiArna
NicholsMarilynMonroe
LinusTorvalds
SpielbergAndyWarhol
hyJoel RuPaul
HarveyWeinsteinJaquelineKennedyUnas
JimBakkerLucyLawlessMuhammadAli
AndyKaufmanJackKerouac KarlRov
EdWoodJr.CondoleezzaRice StephenHaw
HowardStern50CentRobertRedford
ChrisRockWayneHuizengaJackWhite

Also by Brad Dunn

New York: The Unknown City

When They Were 22

MattDrudge DianeSa...
zKafkaF.ScottFitzgerald Mr. ...
kyDr.Seuss RobertRedford
dyGuthrieStanleyKubrick Curtis
yHepburn DavidHasselhoff
nani Estée Lauder
StephenH... RichardBransonSe...
HunterS.Thompson
DianeSawyerSh...
coChanelJerryGarci...
RobertCrumb
amieFoxxNorahJonesS...
DavidBowieJerry
GarnerJanisJoplin
J.EdgarHoover
Cash DorothyParker
ohnBelushiPamelaAnderson
elaceRaymondCarverRobertAltman
SeanConnery JerryFalwell
y"CombsRingoStarrErnestHeming
ewinskyBradPittAnselAdams

OprahWinfreyCheech
RalphNader MalcolmXEliot
BillMurraySusanSarandon
onsSandraDayO'Connor GarthBrook
RoseanneBarr FrankZappa RodSerli
J.D.Salinger RonaldReagan
riciaCornwellJim HelenKelle
SissySpacek
ChristieBrinkleyZap
aronStoneHowardSt
SteveMartin
AliceWalkerDesiArna
NicholsMarilynMonroe
LinusTorvalds
SpielbergAndyWarhol
nyJoel RuPaul
HarveyWeinsteinJaquelineKennedyUnas
JimBakkerLucyLawlessMuhammadAli
AndyKaufmanJackKerouacKarlRov
EdWoodJr.CondoleezzaRice StephenHawk
HowardStern50CentRobertRedford
ChrisRockWayneHuizengaJackWhite

100 Famous People at the Turning Point in Their Lives **Brad Dunn**

Andrews McMeel
Publishing

Kansas City

06 07 08 09 10 FFG 10 9 8 7 6 5 4 3 2

ISBN-13: 978-0-7407-5810-2

ISBN-10: 0-7407-5810-1

Library of Congress Cataloging-in-Publication Data

Dunn, Brad, 1973-
   When they were 22 : 100 famous people at the turning point in their lives
     / Brad Dunn.
     p. cm.
   Includes bibliographical references.
   ISBN-13: 978-0-7407-5810-2
   ISBN-10: 0-7407-5810-1
    1. Celebrities--Biography. 2. Biography--20th century. 3. Life change
      events. I. Title.

CT120.D855 2006
920.009'04--dc22
[B]

2005057170

Design: Jim Walsh, Kansas City, Missouri

For Amy, with love and stroller

Contents

Introduction

Most of us can point to one or two times in our lives when everything changed, when a single decision or chance encounter forever altered the future.

It could be a romance (as it was for F. Scott Fitzgerald), a fender bender (Marilyn Monroe), an acid trip (Robert Crumb), or a series of electroshock treatments (Larry Flynt). Jane Goodall's life was changed by a trip to Africa; for Harrison Ford, it was a trip to the men's room.

These pivotal moments are the most fascinating part of any biography because they reveal the unexpected turning points in life and lay bare the incredible process of human destiny.

Where a biography tracks one life through many moments, this book follows many lives through one moment. These are portraits of famous people—actors, politicians, writers, criminals, porn stars—at the most pivotal time in their lives.

If you look for that turning point across a spectrum of personalities, you'll find a recurring theme: age 22. No other age contains more risks, more big decisions, more random strokes of fate. Like Fitzgerald, Flynt, and Ford, more people experience life-altering changes at 22 than at any other point in their lives.

Of course, some find their callings much earlier. Albert Einstein is not in this book. Neither is Bob Dylan, or Katharine Hepburn, or Michael Jordan. They all discovered their talents at a younger age and by 22 were developing another theorem, recording another album, starring in another movie, or signing another contract with the Chicago Bulls.

But for the people in this book, and for most of us, the path was not so clear so early. Instead, we see Bill Murray studying to become a surgeon and Pamela Anderson teaching an aerobics class. Matt Drudge worked in a gift shop; Jack White was an upholsterer. Yet, all of them share one thing: a personal metamorphosis at 22.

If you've been there, you'll remember what that age is like: filled with excitement and uncertainty, vague ambitions struggling to find definition. Endless possibilities line the horizon—enough to inspire you or to paralyze you with indecision.

If you haven't reached that age yet, the stories in this book will give you a glimpse of the vast and unpredictable roads that lie ahead.

Ronald Reagan found success after a string of failures: "At twenty-two I'd achieved my dream: I was a sports announcer. If I had stopped there, I believe I would have been happy the rest of my life," he said. Oprah Winfrey found failure after a string of successes: "I was called in and put on the edge of being fired . . . I was devastated. I was twenty-two and embarrassed . . . because I had never failed before," she recalled. Yet, for both of them, 22 marked a radical turning point in their lives.

Some people discover a new world at that age: Woody Guthrie, Raquel Welch, and Brad Pitt all packed up for Los Angeles. Others have to hit rock bottom first: Billy Joel tried to kill himself by drinking a bottle of furniture polish.

These are portraits of young people at the crossroads, making bold decisions, suffering early defeats, reveling in unexpected triumphs. Some are in a rut. Some are hell-bent on success. Some get lucky. Some get blindsided by misfortune.

But they're in this book because they ultimately did something remarkable with their lives, and to understand their story, you only need to glimpse them at their most defining moment: age 22.

Join the Club

Ansel Adams turned 22 on February 20, 1924.

One of the most celebrated photographers in the history of the camera grew up hoping to make a living using his ear, not his eye.

Born and raised in San Francisco, Ansel Adams taught himself to play piano at age 12 and dreamed of becoming a concert performer.* He even quit school to pursue music full-time. In his late teens, however, he made his first trip to Yosemite National Park and was awestruck by the grandeur and beauty of the Sierra Nevada. He returned home and begged his parents to get him a camera so he could capture all the outdoor splendors he'd seen. They bought him one, and Adams's time on the piano bench rapidly declined.

Toting his Kodak No. 1 Box Brownie, Adams hiked, camped, climbed, and snapped hundreds of photographs of the park, which he used as records of his journeys. He joined the Sierra Club and spent four summers as the keeper of its LeConte Memorial Lodge. The club published regular bulletins, and in 1924 Adams saw a chance to turn his photography pastime into professional work.

The summer after his 22nd birthday, he set up camp in his makeshift darkroom and created his first significant photographs. His dedication paid off and spurred a major turning point in his life. The Sierra Club agreed to publish several of his pictures in its bulletin that fall. The photos received instant and widespread praise for their stark contrast and mesmerizing depth. Adams had found his calling.

He became a regular contributor to the bulletin until 1928, when he had accumulated enough work to open his own exhibition at the Sierra Club's headquarters in San Francisco. The show garnered national attention and inspired him to devote the rest of his life to photography and conservation.

*See Jamie Foxx, page 44, and Condoleezza Rice, page 119.

Champ Revamped

Muhammad Ali turned 22 on January 17, 1964.

Perhaps the greatest athlete of the twentieth century, the boxer born as Cassius Clay not only became heavyweight champion of the world at age 22 but he also adopted a new religion* and reinvented his identity.

After winning a gold medal in the 1960 Summer Olympics in Rome, Clay took his unorthodox boxing style—and penchant for self-promotion—to the professional circuit. Though the Louisville, Kentucky, native was an underachiever in school, he proved to be extremely intelligent and quick-witted with reporters. He soon became known as the "Louisville Lip" for his rhyming taunts and outrageous boasts. "I am the greatest," he said. "Not only do I knock 'em out, I pick the round!"

Clay backed up his bravado: By the end of 1963, his record was 19 wins, 0 losses, with 15 knockouts, and he was the top contender for Sonny Liston's heavyweight title. Although Liston was the Mike Tyson of his day, an intimidating fighter who appeared invincible, Clay taunted him mercilessly in the press. "He's too ugly to be the champ!" he shouted. When he learned bookies had set odds against him at 8 to 1, Clay retorted, "If you wanna lose your money, then bet on Sonny."

He even wrote a poem about the bout, in which he predicted he'd punch Liston so hard, the heavyweight would fly out of the ring:

Now Liston disappears from view, the crowd's getting frantic,
But our radar station's picked him up over the Atlantic.
Who would have thought when they came to the fight,
That they'd witness the launching of a human satellite?
Yes, the crowd did not dream, when they laid down their money,
That they would see a total eclipse of the Sonny.

During the weigh-in before the Miami fight, Clay famously declared that he would "float like a butterfly, sting like a bee" and even named the round he would win: "To prove I'm great, he will fall in eight." Still, few believed the brash young boxer stood a chance of beating the powerful Liston.

But on February 25, 1964, a month after his 22nd birthday, Clay pulled off one of the most astonishing upsets in boxing history. After suffering partial blindness in the fifth round (some accused Liston of smearing his gloves with an oil), Clay recovered and went on to win the fight in the seventh—when Liston surrendered.

Though the victory marked a turning point in Clay's life, it was only the beginning. The next day, the new champ shocked the boxing world again: He announced that he had accepted the teachings of the Nation of Islam** and had dropped his "slave name" Cassius Clay and would now go by Cassius X. In the same way that Malcolm Little had recast himself as Malcolm X, Clay said the X symbolized the unknown name of his African ancestors that whites had taken away from him.

A few weeks later, however, the boxer announced that his spiritual mentor Elijah Muhammad had given him a new name, Muhammad Ali, and that he was planning a trip to Mecca. He reasserted that his decision to convert to Islam was the product of months of study, and that the Nation of Islam preached "the truth and light": "A rooster crows only when it sees the light," he said. "Put him in the dark and he'll never crow. I have seen the light and I'm crowing."

As Ali went on to become one of the greatest boxers in history, his religious views changed along the way. In the 1970s he rigorously studied the Koran, converted to Sunni Islam, and rejected the Nation of Islam.

*See Bob Marley, page 96.
**See Malcolm X, page 91.

Gone to the Dogs

Robert Altman turned 22 on February 20, 1947.

If a bizarre business scheme hadn't failed him when he was 22 years old, Robert Altman might never have become a legendary filmmaker. Having served as a copilot in the U.S. Army Air Forces during World War II, Altman made a fateful trip to a pet store when he was discharged: "Right after the war I got a dog for myself. I don't know why, it was a terrible bull terrier," Altman once said. "The guy I bought it from had this thing called an Identicode, which he would tattoo onto dogs for identification. I thought this was a terrific idea."

Altman saw the device as a potential money-maker, and he formed a dog-tattooing company with the pet store owner. Altman was vice president. The pair traveled the country offering to tattoo canines, either inside the leg or behind the ear, with unique serial numbers that would go into a national database. If the dog were ever lost, animal shelters could identify the pet's owner.

Altman poured all of his energy into the endeavor and soon hatched a wild publicity stunt. A Kansas City native, he used his family contacts in Missouri to arrange a meeting with President Harry Truman. The commander in chief was so impressed with the Identicode, he allowed Altman to use it on his dog. The young war veteran traveled to Washington and in front of cameras and reporters proudly tattooed the president's cocker spaniel, Feller.

Business shot up after all the media attention. But, soon enough, the demand for animal tattoos all but vanished. "We thought we were off to be millionaires," Altman said. "It turned out that I just got a few dog bites."

While he was flying bombing missions in the Pacific during the war, Altman had daydreamed about writing radio plays and screenplays. With little hope left of striking it rich on dogs tattoos, the 22-year-old decided to try his luck at a new career: filmmaking.

He sold the business at a small profit and joined Kansas City's Calvin Company, one of the country's top producers of industrial short films. Altman learned the trade and went on to make dozens of educational films.

In 1970, he directed a feature film that made him an overnight celebrity; the wartime black comedy *M*A*S*H* also got him his first Oscar nomination. He directed several other influential movies, including *Nashville*, *The Player*, *Short Cuts*,* and *Gosford Park*. He has been nominated for seven Academy Awards, but has never won.

When asked if he regretted giving up the dog-tattooing business for show business, Altman said, "Well, they're both about the same."

*See Raymond Carver, page 19.

Curves in the Crowd

Pamela Anderson turned 22 on July 1, 1989.

Pamela Anderson made two decisions at age 22 that permanently changed the course of her life. She got her first breast implants and she wore an extremely form-fitting Labatt's beer T-shirt to a Canadian football game.

Of course, a bit of luck also helped: While a cameraman was panning across the stadium during a break in play, he stopped on the buxom blonde. When her image was shown on the giant screen, the stadium erupted in cheers. The reaction was so strong that Anderson was escorted down to the fifty-yard line, where she grabbed a microphone and introduced herself to the crowd. An executive at Labatt's beer saw what everyone else saw: a jaw-dropping blonde whose figure could captivate a crowd. He sent out agents to find her and sign her up for a new ad campaign.

Anderson, the soon-to-be-renowned Labatt's "Blue Zone" girl, already had small tastes of success under her belt. In fact, her first brush with fame happened at her birth: She was the first baby born on the 100th anniversary of Canada's independence, July 1, 1967, and was hailed as the "Centennial Baby." "It all started there," Anderson once said.

Her first modeling job came in first grade, when a photographer picked her out of a crowd of 100 children at a library reading. People loved the image of the smiley little girl so much that the library copyrighted it and published it throughout British Columbia. She later landed bit parts in movies shot in Canada, including *Crimes of Passion* and *Some Kind of Wonderful*. In her high school yearbook, she said she'd like to "be a California beach bum." Anderson's desire to make it big prompted her to move at age 20 away from her small town and to Vancouver, where she got a job as a fitness instructor.

But it was the Labatt's ad campaign that sent her on her way.

The posters and billboards were so successful that a photographer convinced Anderson to send pictures of herself to *Playboy* magazine. The editors there liked what they saw: A few months after her 22nd birthday, Anderson flew to Los Angeles to do a photo shoot at the Playboy Mansion.

After a self-conscious start (Anderson wouldn't take her clothes off), she soon hit her stride and by the end of the session had lost herself in the moment. "I was shooting so many rolls of film that they had to stop me from walking out into the street naked," Anderson said.

Her appearance on the cover of *Playboy* in October 1989 sparked a series of breakthroughs. ABC recruited her for a regular role on the TV show *Home Improvement*, where she played Lisa, the Tool Time girl. In turn, David Hasselhoff spotted her on the sitcom and asked if she would like to star in *Baywatch*, his new series.*

In 1992, three years after she attended a Canadian football game, Pamela Anderson was introduced to a global audience as C. J. Parker, a sexy blonde lifeguard and constant scene-stealer in one of the most popular syndicated shows in history.

See David Hasselhoff, page 54.

Shopping for a Career

Giorgio Armani turned 22 on July 11, 1956.

Before he became one of the world's foremost fashion designers, Giorgio Armani wanted to be a photographer—and before that a doctor. His whirlwind of career aspirations ended at age 22, however, when he decided to take a job at a department store.

Born and raised in Piacenza, Italy, Armani enrolled in medical school at age 18 aspiring to become a surgeon.* But when he was called to military service two years later and worked as an army paramedic, he realized medicine was not his calling. He returned home and gave professional photography a try but quickly determined he wasn't talented enough to make a living at it.

Shortly after his 22nd birthday, Armani was looking for work and managed to land a job as a window dresser at La Rinascente, Milan's high-end department store. He became fascinated by the marketing side of the fashion business. When a manager recognized Armani's eye for style and offered him a promotion, he jumped at the chance. Within months, he was one of the store's top buyers of menswear, amazing his supervisors by acquiring cutting-edge fashions that flew off the racks.

After working several years as a designer, he went out on his own in 1970 and launched the Giorgio Armani brand—which became one of the most sought-after labels in the world.

*See Bill Murray, page 103.

Riches to Rags

Desi Arnaz turned 22 on March 2, 1939.

As a teenager, Desiderio Alberto Arnaz y de Acha III had a life about as regal as his name. The future *I Love Lucy* star's father was the mayor of Santiago, Cuba, and the family lived luxuriously at their mansion, three ranches, and private island. But when the Batista revolution toppled the government in 1933, the Arnaz family lost everything and fled to the United States.

Desi Arnaz had to adjust to a much humbler life in Miami. He realized he wouldn't get anywhere without speaking English, so he studied rigorously while trying to make money for the family however he could: driving taxis, busing tables, cleaning birdcages at a pet store. His most significant odd job, however, began after he bought a $5 guitar at a pawn shop. A gifted musician and lifelong lover of Cuban music, Arnaz joined a rumba band that played at fancy hotels on Miami Beach. He enjoyed the music scene so much that he formed his own band.

Just as Latin-Cuban rhythms were gaining popularity across the country, Arnaz, at age 22, made a decision that forever shaped his future: He started playing the conga drums. His Miami audiences fell in love with the new sound, and soon the "conga line" dance craze swept the country.

In 1939, Arnaz and his La Conga Orchestra were invited to play in New York, where the handsome Cuban not only electrified audiences with his big-band style and rousing vocals, but also drew the attention of several Broadway producers. Arnaz was cast in the Rodgers and Hart musical *Too Many Girls*. The show was a smash, and when RKO executives bought the film rights, they signed Arnaz to reprise his stage role in the movie.

It was on the set that the 22-year-old conga player met actress Lucille Ball, six years his senior. The two launched a turbulent courtship that culminated in a secret wedding six months later.

The union became one of the most legendary in Hollywood history, leading not only to one of the most beloved sitcoms of the 1950s, *I Love Lucy*, but also to the creation of Desilu Studios, one of the most successful television production companies of all time.

Touched by Tammy Faye

Jim Bakker turned 22 on January 2, 1961.

The popular televangelist whose scandalous downfall made headlines around the world in the 1980s started his ministry after meeting the woman of his dreams at age 22.

James Orson met Tammy Faye Bakker in the spring of 1961 at North Central Bible College. The Muskegon, Michigan, native found his perfect match in the young woman: Both had grown up in extremely poor families and both wanted to devote their lives to the service of God. He soon married his sweetheart and decided to take her last name.*

By the end of 1961, the Bakkers made a living as traveling preachers, hopping from church to church, where he would deliver impassioned sermons and she would play hymns on the accordion. They developed a reputation for their spirited Sunday school shows for children, in which Tammy Faye worked puppets, while Jim narrated Christian lessons.

Within four years, the couple attracted enough attention that renowned evangelist Pat Robertson invited them to join his up-and-coming Christian Broadcasting Network. In 1966, the Bakkers launched *The PTL (Praise the Lord) Club,* which remained one of the most popular television ministries until its collapse in 1987 amid adultery and fraud charges. Jim Bakker went to prison for five years, prompting fellow evangelist Jerry Falwell** to brand him a liar, an embezzler, a sexual deviate, and "the greatest scab and cancer on the face of Christianity in two thousand years of church history."

*See Jack White, page 166.
**See Jerry Falwell, page 35.

The Customer's Always Right

Roseanne Barr turned 22 on November 3, 1974.

She was such a surly and sarcastic waitress, many customers told her she should take her working-class shtick to the comedy circuit. At age 22, that's exactly what Roseanne Barr did—and the move forever changed her life.

She grew up in a lower-middle-class family in Salt Lake City and not long after dropping out of high school got married and moved to an artists' colony outside Denver. She had three children and helped make ends meet by working part-time as a waitress. Her caustic remarks to customers and coworkers and her impromptu monologues about the trials of domestic life got lots of laughs —and tips.

After endless encouragement to try stand-up, she finally got up her nerve, put together a routine, and hit the comedy clubs in downtown Denver in 1975. She was a huge success and became one of the most popular comedians in Colorado. In the early 1980s, she was invited to perform at the Comedy Store in Los Angeles. The exposure led to an appearance on *The Tonight Show* and two HBO specials. She launched her award-winning sitcom *Roseanne* in 1988, a show that stayed at the top of the rankings throughout its nine-year run.

Prodigal Son

John Belushi turned 22 on January 24, 1971.

His father pressured him to join the family restaurant business, but John Belushi's resistance at age 22 left him poised for the break of a lifetime.

Born in Chicago, raised in Wheaton, Illinois, Belushi was an outstanding football player in high school and wanted to turn professional or pursue a coaching career. But his drama teacher told him he had a gift for physical comedy, and the idea took root. After graduation, Belushi performed in summer stock, usually playing—or deliberately overplaying—the fool. When he dropped out of college, his father insisted that he become a partner in his restaurant, but Belushi repeatedly declined. He had concocted another plan.

He had always admired the infamous Second City* comedy troupe in Chicago. Not long after his 22nd birthday, he decided to launch his own improv group, the West Compass Players, which performed at small clubs in Wheaton and Glen Ellyn. The troupe attracted a following and in the spring of 1971, Belushi was invited to join Second City.

During his rigorous six-nights-a-week performance schedule, he honed his loudmouthed, gonzo style of comedy and became particularly famous for his dead-on impression of pop musician Joe Cocker, with his trademark intensity and exaggerated facial tics. Belushi also once did an impression of Hamlet, serious and brooding, saying: "To be . . . to be sure beats the shit out of not to be."

After he left Second City in 1972, Belushi was cast in the Off-Broadway comedy *Lemmings*, where he met Chevy Chase. In 1975, he was chosen as a member of the first cast of *Saturday Night Live*.

*See Mike Nichols, page 108, and Bill Murray, page 103.

Lost in Space

David Bowie turned 22 on January 8, 1969.

If he hadn't seen *2001: A Space Odyssey*, David Bowie probably wouldn't have written a song at age 22 that permanently altered his life.

The musical prodigy who grew up playing saxophone, guitar, and piano dabbled in many music styles, including blues, folk, and rock, but had no luck making a name for himself in the early 1960s. He even changed his name to increase his chances. Born David Jones, he was afraid of being confused with Davy Jones, the lead singer of the Monkees. In 1966, he took on a new handle in honor of Alamo hero Jim Bowie and his renowned Bowie knife.

In 1967, Bowie thought he'd finally gotten his break when Deram Records signed him for a solo album. Unfortunately, *David Bowie*, an odd mix of pop and psychedelic tracks,* sold poorly and he was dropped from the label.

Frustrated by a slew of false starts, the struggling artist abandoned music altogether and retreated to a Buddhist monastery in Scotland, where he studied to become a monk under guru Chime Yong Dong Rinpoche. "After a few months of study, he told me, 'You don't want to be Buddhist,'" Bowie once recalled. "He said, 'You should follow music.'"

Bowie returned to London but this time with a new artistic vision: He wanted to be a mime. He joined Lindsay Kemp's famous mime troupe and learned the art. He enjoyed it so much, in 1968 he formed his own experimental mixed-media company, The Feathers. Here, Bowie not only mimed, but also painted, acted, danced, sang, and wrote plays.

Again success eluded him. The Feathers attracted very small audiences, and finally the troupe broke up. A few weeks before his 22nd birthday, a depressed Bowie saw Stanley Kubrick's** masterpiece *2001: A Space Odyssey*. The film, about an astronaut who undergoes a dazzling transformation in space, seemed to speak directly to Bowie's feelings of isolation and desire for change. "I always had a repulsive need to be something more than human," he said.

The movie inspired him to compose "Space Oddity," a ballad about an astronaut, Major Tom, who becomes lost in space and loses communication with Earth. Bowie's girlfriend and soon-to-be wife, Angela Barnett, convinced a friend at Mercury Records to listen to the song. With NASA planning to send a man to the moon that summer, Mercury decided "Space Oddity" was perfect for the times. It released the single right before the July 20, 1969, moon landing, and the BBC even aired the song during its coverage of the historical event.

After years of disappointment, the stars finally aligned for Bowie. When "Space Oddity" hit No. 5 on the British charts, Mercury wanted a full album. Bowie recorded songs for *Man of Words, Man of Music*, later reissued as *Space Oddity*, which was a sensation on both sides of the Atlantic.

Bowie became a pioneer of glam rock in the 1970s and went on to release a series of successful albums, including *The Rise and Fall of Ziggy Stardust and the Spiders from Mars*.

*See Billy Joel, page 68.
**See Stanley Kubrick, page 83.

Follow the Money

Richard Branson turned 22 on July 18, 1972.

"I wanted to be an editor or a journalist, I wasn't really interested in being an entrepreneur," billionaire Richard Branson once said. "But I soon found I had to become an entrepreneur in order to keep my magazine going."

That magazine was called *Student*, a youth-culture chronicle for the baby boomers of England. Branson started publishing at age 16 while attending the Stowe School in London and kept it afloat until his early 20s. To augment his revenue, he started a mail-order record company in 1970. But at age 22, Branson realized he'd have to take the entrepreneurial effort a step further to pay the bills—so he rebranded his small business and launched Virgin Records.

He opened a recording studio on Oxford Street and signed his first artist: Mike Oldfield. The multitalented musician played twenty instruments on his—and Virgin's—debut album, *Tubular Bells*. But Branson's hunch was right: Oldfield's progressive rock sound found wide appeal on both sides of the Atlantic. The album sold 5 million copies and flooded the 22-year-old's new business with cash.

He soon signed what would become the biggest acts of the 1970s and 80s: the Sex Pistols, Boy George and Culture Club, and Simple Minds, as well as rock legends the Rolling Stones and Genesis. From there, Branson branched off into several other businesses, including airlines, cosmetics, and phone services.

One Sick Puppy

Christie Brinkley turned 22 on February 2, 1976.

Christie Brinkley owes her three-decade modeling career to an ailing dog. The photogenic blonde says she never set out to become a supermodel but instead grew up dreaming of an artist's lifestyle. Her father, Don Brinkley, was a successful television producer and often brought Christie down to the studio to watch the actors. "It was fabulous," she remembered. "But I was determined that I was going to live in Paris and be an artist."

After learning to speak French fluently at Le Lycée Français de Los Angeles, she moved to Paris* at age 18. Within a year, she had fallen in love and married an artist, Jean-François Allaux. She also found work as an entry-level illustrator, drawing things such as "little travel maps with elephants in India and flamingos in Florida" for airline companies.

Young, in Paris, and in love, Brinkley was living her dream. Not long after her 22nd birthday, however, two strokes of fate combined to change the course of her life.

First, her dog became sick and she was unable to pay the growing stack of veterinary bills. Second, she was spotted at random by a photographer who told her she had the right look for modeling. He offered to snap some portfolio shots. Eager to make money, she accepted.** Within weeks, she was discovered by the Ford Agency.

The formerly struggling artist was shocked at her first paycheck, which more than covered the vet bills. "I did one job, and I couldn't believe the money," she said. "I thought, 'Wow.'"

At age 22, Brinkley signed a twenty-year contract with Cover Girl cosmetics (an industry record) and gained worldwide renown by posing on the cover of *Sports Illustrated's* swimsuit issue three years in a row (another record) starting in 1979.

*See Robert Redford, page 117.
**See Marilyn Monroe, page 101.

"A Big Bell Went Off"

Garth Brooks turned 22 on February 7, 1984.

Country singer Garth Brooks had a life-changing epiphany while lying on a high-jump mat during his senior year in college.

The 22-year-old had won a track-and-field scholarship for the javelin throw but during his final semester failed to qualify for a championship competition. "I'm laying there on the high-jump mat, just disappointed as hell," he once recalled. "And that's when a big bell went off and said, 'Hey, man, you're terrible at athletics, you're terrible at college. But the one thing you're proud to put your name to is your music. Maybe that's what the good Lord wants you to do.'"

Born in Tulsa, Oklahoma, Brooks grew up in a musical family, learned guitar in his teens, and sang pop and country songs. But sports dominated his early life, and when he was recruited by Oklahoma State University, he decided to study advertising while trying to make it as an athlete.

A few months after his 22nd birthday, however, Brooks had a scuttled sports career, a bachelor's degree in advertising, and no career aspirations. He decided to give country music a chance. Having played guitar with his roommate Ty England throughout college, he convinced his friend to play with him at roadhouse bars around Stillwater, Oklahoma. The duo gained a steady following and ultimately became the house band at a bar called Wet Willie's. The regular gigs inspired him to devote his life to music.

Brooks got up the nerve to go to Nashville in 1985, and though he was initially rejected,* he persevered and won a recording contract with Capitol Records three years later. His debut self-titled album came out in April 1989 and gave Brooks his first top ten single, "Much Too Young (to Feel This Damn Old)," that summer.

*See Johnny Cash, page 20.

The Key to Writing

Raymond Carver turned 22 on May 25, 1960.

The short story writer acclaimed for his minimalism, realism, and repeated struggles with alcohol not only published his first story at age 22, but also met the literary mentor that shaped his life's work.

Raymond Carver was a married father of two by the time he was 20, and though he held down an array of blue-collar jobs to pay the bills, he also devoted time to his ultimate dream of becoming a writer. In 1958, he moved his family from Yakima, Washington, to Paradise, California, so he could take creative-writing classes at Chico State College. It was there he met the author and professor John Gardner. "He offered me the key to his office," Carver later wrote. "I see that gift now as a turning point."

Gardner saw enormous potential in the young writer and gave his student intense line-by-line critiques of his work. He taught Carver that literature should not be a form of self-expression, but a form of communication. He despised the cynicism of the early 1960s and impressed upon Carver the idea that the greatest art is not nihilistic, but life-affirming. He also told him that great writing is not a product of a flurry of emotions, but of painstaking rewrites and revisions. Carver said that throughout his life, every time he wrote he felt Gardner looking over his shoulder.

At age 22, the aspiring writer finally finished a short story he felt was suitable for publication. "The Furious Seasons" was published in the spring of 1961 in the college literary review *Selection*. The experience thrilled Carver and redoubled his desire to write.

Although he continued to impress readers and editors, he did not become a nationally known author until 1971, when *Esquire* published his story "Neighbors." Carver's stories were the basis for Robert Altman's* 1993 critically acclaimed film *Short Cuts*.

See Robert Altman, page 4.

Sun Rise

Johnny Cash turned 22 on February 26, 1954.

Music legend Johnny Cash experienced more changes at age 22 than many people do in a lifetime. In one year, he went from decoding Russian communications at a German base near the Iron Curtain to recording his first country single at Sun Records in Memphis, Tennessee—and he got married, went back to school, sold appliances door-to-door, and suffered considerable rejection along the way.

Born to poor Arkansas sharecroppers during the Depression, Cash grew up working in cotton fields and listening to country crooners on the radio. "That was the big thing when I was growing up, singing on the radio," Cash once said. "The extent of my dream was to sing on the radio station in Memphis."

After high school, Cash hitchhiked to Pontiac, Michigan, where he got a job at an auto factory. But when the Korean War started, he enlisted in the Air Force and was shipped out to Landsberg, Germany.

Cash proved so talented at deciphering enemy Morse code messages that he was made a radio-intercept operator and assigned to monitor the Russians. One of his lesser-known distinctions: Cash was the first Westerner to learn of Joseph Stalin's death in 1953 because he intercepted and decoded a communiqué sent to Moscow.

Cash's military pay of $85 a month was a fortune to him. He made the first luxury purchase of his life at the PX, a $5 guitar, and then taught himself how to play scores of old tunes. "All through the Air Force, I was so lonely," Cash said. "If I couldn't have sung all those old country songs, I don't think I could have made it."

He also wrote his first song in Germany after seeing a movie called *Inside the Walls of Folsom Prison*. Cash tried to imagine the thoughts of some unrepentant inmate, a murderer, perhaps, who had "shot a man in Reno, just to watch him die." He also formed his first band, the Landsberg Barbarians.

But when he was discharged a few months after his 22nd birthday, Cash returned home and concentrated on laying roots and building a home. He married Vivian Liberto, whom he'd met in Texas during basic training, and then migrated to Memphis, where he enrolled to study radio announcing at the Keegan School of Broadcasting under the GI Bill. His older brother Roy got him a job selling home appliances door-to-door to help make ends meet.

Although he struggled to find a job as a radio announcer—he was turned away at every station he tried—Cash continued to dream of being a professional singer. He even formed a band with two men he met through his brother, guitarist Luther Perkins and bassist Marshall Grant. The trio practiced at night and performed gospel songs at Sunday church events.

Finally losing interest in radio announcing, Cash staked everything on becoming a performer. But opportunities were scarce.* After failing to persuade local radio managers to let him play during live shows, Cash worked up the courage to visit the renowned Sun Records studio, hoping to land an audition. "I went and knocked on that door and was turned away," Cash said. "I called back for an interview three or four times, was turned away."

Cash camped out at the studio's entrance and finally talked producer Cowboy Jack Clement into letting him play a song. Clement was impressed enough to invite Cash back to play for Sam Phillips, the famous producer who discovered Elvis Presley, Jerry Lee Lewis, and Carl Perkins.

Cash played mostly gospel songs at his audition, and Phillips, known for not mincing words, didn't like what he heard. He told Cash to "go home and sin, then come back with a song I can sell."

Cash did as he was told. He and his band returned with "Hey Porter," a frenetic tune that won Phillips over. A week after his

23rd birthday, Cash recorded it for a single, along with "Cry, Cry, Cry." The release sold well and Phillips signed Cash and his band, the Tennessee Two, to a recording contract that ultimately led to "Folsom Prison Blues" and "I Walk the Line," two hits that secured Cash's place in country music.

When asked years later about his audition at Sun Records, Cash said, "If there hadn't been a Sam Phillips, I might still be working in a cotton field."

*See Garth Brooks, page 18.

Café Romance

Coco Chanel turned 22 on August 19, 1905.

The preeminent fashion designer who created the little black dress and Chanel No. 5 perfume started off life in an orphanage and took an odd job at age 22 that proved pivotal to her future.

Born Gabrielle Chanel in Saumur, France, she learned to sew at age 10 to make spare change at the orphanage in which she and her four siblings resided, and went to work full-time as a seamstress assistant in her teens. She became an expert at trimming ladies' hats but was forced to labor in abysmal work conditions and barely made enough money to live on.

A few months after her 22nd birthday, she decided to start singing in cafés on the side. Her petite figure and canary-like voice earned her the nickname "Coco," which means "darling" and "little pet," and she became well known for her versions of popular songs that played on her nickname, including "Ko Ko Ri Ko" and "Who's Seen Coco in the Trocadero?"

In the spring of 1906, however, the course of her life changed when a wealthy bachelor named Etienne Balsan noticed her and fell in love. Chanel soon quit her seamstress work, moved out of her modest apartment, and took up residence at Balsan's country estate. She was fascinated by the lives of courtesans but was puzzled why upper-class women dressed in clothes that appeared to be designed for men. At 22, she had her first vision of a style of clothing that would revolutionize women's fashion.

Within a few years, she convinced Balsan to let her turn his Paris pied-à-terre into a clothing shop. She worked tirelessly creating sleek, sexy, form-fitting clothes for women. Her designs were so sought-after that by the 1920s she had turned her small shop into a major hub of haute couture—and started setting the styles that would influence a century of fashions.

In the Right Hands

Tracy Chapman turned 22 on March 30, 1986.

The bluesy folk singer who burst on the scene in the late 1980s and won four Grammy Awards owes much of her success to a college classmate who happened to overhear her music.

While majoring in anthropology and African studies at Tufts University, Chapman took her guitar to coffeehouses around Medford, Massachusetts, and played at open-mike nights. The Cleveland native had grown up practicing guitar and imitating early blues and folk singers. She had been writing songs since her teens.

When she was 22, she recorded a demo tape at the student-run radio station and passed copies around to friends. One tape landed in the hands of Brian Koppelman, a future screenwriter and son of Charles Koppelman, then-president of the music company SBK Publishing. Brian liked Chapman's crisp sound and poignant lyrics so much that he encouraged his father to give her a listen.

The elder Koppelman saw the same potential in the 22-year-old. He got her a managing contract with Elliot Roberts, who had worked with Neil Young and Joni Mitchell. Chapman spent the summer after her graduation recording songs and by early 1987, had landed a record contract with Elektra.

Her self-titled debut album hit stores a year later and produced a chart-topping single, "Fast Car." The album went platinum and earned Chapman critical praise across the country.

Concert Catastrophe

Sean "Diddy" Combs turned 22 on November 4, 1991.

Sean Combs's promising start in the hip-hop industry was nearly ruined by tragedy. At 21, he was the golden child at a major rap label. But at 22, all fingers pointed at him after nine people were crushed to death at a rap concert. He was fired from his job and, friends say, paralyzed with grief over the tragedy. His rising star appeared to have vanished.

Born in Harlem, New York, Combs experienced tragedy early when his father was gunned down in Central Park. Combs was 3 years old. When he was 12, his mother moved the family north of the city to Mount Vernon and enrolled him in an all-boys school. He got good enough grades to go to Howard University in Washington, D.C., where his entrepreneurial spirit soared. He not only promoted house parties and concerts, but also reportedly made a lot of money selling old exams and term papers on the side.

The fast track wasn't fast enough for Combs, and after two years, he dropped out of college, returned to New York, and angled for work at a hip-hop label. He landed an internship at Uptown Records, where he helped produce several hit singles, including Jodeci's 1991 "Forever My Lady." The owner was so impressed with Combs's talent that he advanced the intern to vice president of promotions. While his friends were graduating from Howard, Combs was already heir apparent to a major record label.

But all that changed on December 28, 1991.

Combs had dreamed up a charity basketball game/rap concert in Harlem, and got Mike Tyson and other celebrities to sign on. He aggressively promoted the event on radio and in newspapers. He attracted so much interest that on the night of the concert, more than 5,000 people lined up outside the 2,700–capacity gymnasium. When someone closed the entrance and blocked it with a table, hundreds of ticket holders feared they weren't going to get in. A throng of angry fans broke through the entrance and poured into a small lobby where the doors to the gym had been shut. As the crowd pressed in, nine were crushed to death and twenty-seven were injured.

Combs himself was in the riot and was one of the last people to make it into the gym before people started getting trampled. He later testified that he turned around and saw the faces of people getting crushed. "You could see panic on everybody's face," he said. But differing accounts surfaced about Combs's involvement that night. Some witnesses said they saw him giving first aid to the victims. Others said they saw him casually counting money with two women while people were dying.

Though police never filed criminal charges against Combs, investigators said he was to blame for overselling the concert and failing to provide adequate security. Survivors and families of the victims filed several civil suits against him. All were eventually settled out of court but not before a judge excoriated Combs for his role in the tragedy: "It does not take an Einstein to know that young people attending a rap concert camouflaged as a 'celebrity basketball game,' who have paid as much as $20 a ticket, would not be very happy and easy to control if they were unable to gain admission to the event because it was oversold," the judge wrote.

Combs himself testified only once, seven years after the event, and he began by apologizing to the families: "There is not a day that passes that I do not regret the fact that I was a promoter of this tragic event. . . . I have lived with the horror of that night for the last seven years. But my pain is nothing compared to what the victims' families have had to face. I just keep praying that God will give the families the strength to bear it."

At 22, Combs's career in hip-hop seemed to be over. Uptown Records let him go. But after a year, he had already begun to fight his way back in. He produced Mary Blige's album *What's the 411?*

With the proceeds, he formed his own label, Bad Boy Records, and signed rapper Biggie Smalls (aka Notorious BIG).

He went on to become a multimillionaire by producing chart-topping albums and launching his urban clothing line, Sean John.

North Atlantic to
South Pacific

Sean Connery turned 22 on August 25, 1952.

To look at Sean Connery's résumé as a teenager, you would think he was destined for a life of hard manual labor fit for a Dickens novel.

Born to a poor family in Edinburgh, Scotland, Connery dropped out of school at age 13 to help his parents, a truck driver and a charwoman, pay the bills. He sold potatoes and delivered milk and newspapers as a boy, and as he grew stronger became a cement mixer, bricklayer, and steel bender.

He wanted to help his family so much that at age 16, he enlisted in the Royal Navy with the dream of returning home as an officer. As soon as he signed up, he got two tattoos that seemed to reveal everything that was important to him: One read "Scotland Forever," the other "Mum and Dad."

But his laborer's life was already catching up with him. Three years into his Navy stint, Connery was diagnosed with severe peptic ulcers—a condition that has haunted him his whole life—and was discharged with a disability pension.

Back in Edinburgh, Connery decided to formally enter a trade. He studied wood polishing and became an apprentice cabinetmaker. The handsome 20-year-old also ratcheted up his pursuit of women. He started a serious bodybuilding regimen and worked as a lifeguard on weekends to show off his muscles. He also posed in a thong for students at the Edinburgh College of Art.

The Scottish lothario was enjoying life and becoming a respectable tradesman. But he made a decision at 22 that proved to be the turning point in his life.

With his increasingly chiseled body, Connery was encouraged by his trainer to enter the Mr. Universe contest. He accepted the challenge and traveled to London, where he competed in the Tall Man's Division. He won third place. Though the title eluded him, Connery picked up an unexpected prize at the competition: One of his rivals told him that auditions were being held that day for the musical *South Pacific*, which was preparing for a national tour.

Connery tried out on a lark, lied about his theater experience, and won a walk-on role as one of the musclemen in the number "There is Nothin' Like a Dame." He fell in love with theater life. While on tour, he vigorously studied acting and persuaded the producers to let him be an understudy to some of the main actors. Finally, after proving his talents, he won his first acting role, the part of Lt. Buzz Adams, at age 22.

The next year, Connery won parts in the movie *Lilacs in the Spring*, starring Errol Flynn, and the BBC film *Requiem for a Heavyweight*.* Several years later, he landed the role that made him an international celebrity, James Bond, in the 1962 film *Dr. No*.

*See Rod Serling, page 134.

Life of Crime

Patricia Cornwell turned 22 on June 9, 1978.

The author of some of the most popular crime novels of all time —and the person many credit with the popularity of TV shows such as CBS's *CSI: Crime Scene Investigation* and Court TV's *Forensic Files*—landed a job at 22 that set the direction of her life.

After graduating with an English degree from Davidson College in North Carolina, Patricia Cornwell married one of her professors and tried to get a job in journalism. She finally found work at the *Charlotte Observer*, where she was assigned to the police beat.

Cornwell fell in love with crime reporting, and her writing talents appeared immediately: She crafted a series of articles on prostitution and crime in Charlotte that won her an investigative journalism award in 1979. The more she learned about crime-scene analysis, the more she wanted to write about it. In fact, the exposure she had to high-tech police work at age 22 prompted her to switch jobs. "It is important to me to live in the world I write about," she said.

She quit the newspaper and got a position at the Chief Medical Examiner's Office in Virginia. After working for six years as a technical writer, computer analyst, and volunteer police officer, Cornwell wrote her first novel, *Postmortem*—an overnight success that introduced audiences to her reappearing crime sleuth, Dr. Kay Scarpetta.

She went on to write thirteen other Scarpetta novels, as well as a controversial book, *Portrait of a Killer: Jack the Ripper—Case Closed,* on one of the most notorious serial killers in history.

Acid Reign

Robert Crumb turned 22 on August 30, 1965.

"I took some bad acid in November of 1965, and the after-effect left me crazy and helpless for six months," R. Crumb once said. "My direction in life was permanently altered. . . . It was the Road to Damascus for me."

Before Robert Crumb became one of the most revered underground comic artists of the twentieth century—and before he took acid at age 22—the Philadelphia native moved to Cleveland as a teenager and took a job as illustrator for American Greetings. A lifelong sketch artist who grew up worshipping *MAD* magazine, Crumb quickly found his work as a greeting-card designer monotonous. His illustrations started turning creepy, and his boss, future *Ziggy* creator Tom Wilson, insisted he submit drawings that were "less grotesque."

Crumb got married shortly before his 22nd birthday and started submitting comics, including an early version of *Fritz the Cat*, for publication in counterculture magazines. He found enough success to quit his greeting-card job and go to work for *Help!* magazine, where future Monty Python animator Terry Gilliam also worked.

But Crumb was deeply unhappy with his prospects in the comics business and became chronically depressed. His outlook changed, however, when he and his wife started experimenting with LSD.* "It was not yet illegal, and I took it as a sort of substitute for committing suicide," Crumb once said. "The first trip was a completely mystical experience. . . . It completely knocked me off my horse and altered the way I drew. I stopped drawing from life."

Crumb recalled his numerous acid trips during his 22nd year as highly traumatic—full of bizarre side effects and bouts of illness—but also artistically liberating. "My ego was so shattered that it didn't get in the way during what was the most unself-conscious period of my life," he said. "Most of my popular characters—Mr.

Natural, Angelfood McSpade, the Snoid, Shuman the Human, Devil Girl—all suddenly appeared in the drawings in my sketchbook in this period, early 1966."

With a new vision of his life and art, Crumb moved to San Francisco and started drawing comics that captured the booming drug and hippie culture. His provocative and satirical character Mr. Natural, who started appearing on posters and T-shirts with his famous slogan "Keep on Truckin,'" became an icon of the generation.

Crumb also drew art for album covers, including one for Janis Joplin's** band, Big Brother and the Holding Company. In 1967, he launched *Zap Comix*, a publication he handed out on street corners in the Haight-Ashbury area. Crumb is credited with launching the underground comics movement in America.

*See Jerry Garcia, page 45.
**See Janis Joplin, page 73.

Gold in a Trash Can

Matt Drudge turned 22 on October 27, 1988.

While he was failing his way through high school, Matt Drudge often walked the streets alone in Washington, D.C. "Every time, it seemed, I'd end up at the *Washington Post* newsroom on 15th. I'd look up longingly, knowing I'd never get in. Didn't attend the right schools," he once wrote. "My father was not the son of a famous drunken Southern senator, nor was I even remotely connected to a powerful publishing dynasty."

The future Internet news maverick grew up obsessed with current events and political gossip. But after graduating at the bottom of his class in 1984, he frittered away most of his time at menial jobs: He worked the night shift at 7-Eleven, sold Time-Life books over the phone, and was a salesclerk at a grocery store.

Not long after his 22nd birthday, however, Drudge decided he needed a change and made a move that shaped the rest of his life. "In the famous words of another newsman, Horace Greeley: I, still a young man, went West," he said.

Drudge arrived in Los Angeles,* rented a small apartment in Hollywood, and again landed a job as a salesclerk, this time at the gift shop at CBS studios. The self-proclaimed "news junkie" worked his way up to manager and used the job to snoop around the offices hunting for bits of gossip. "I went out of my way to service executive suites, listening carefully to whispered conversation, intercepting the occasional memo. Stalking the newsroom," he recalled. "I hit paydirt when I discovered the trash cans in the Xerox room at Television City." In those trash bins, Drudge found pages and pages of Nielsen ratings, the ultimate yardstick of success on television, before they had been officially released to the public.

Drudge got a computer and started posting the Nielsen ratings —and any other gossip he'd picked up—on Internet newsgroups. He quickly gained a reputation within the growing online news community for having the best "scoops" and juiciest stories.

In 1994, as the Internet was firmly taking hold in households across the nation, he launched the *Drudge Report,* a constantly updated news and gossip Web page. His site gained worldwide fame in 1998 when he posted the story of an affair** between President Bill Clinton and a White House intern.

Though Drudge has suffered criticism from numerous print journalists, his Web site is one of the most frequently visited in the world.

*See Woody Guthrie, page 53, and Brad Pitt, page 114.
**See Monica Lewinsky, page 87.*

Pulled to the Pulpit

Jerry Falwell turned 22 on August 11, 1955.

One of the most outspoken and controversial evangelists of the last century felt the call to become a preacher at age 22.

"I was converted to Jesus Christ on January 20, 1952," Falwell once said. "But I did not know until four years later that God wanted me to be a pastor. My heart was burning to serve Christ. I knew nothing would ever be the same again."

When Falwell found religion at age 18, he was an engineering major at Lynchburg College in his hometown of Lynchburg, Virginia. His conversion was so thorough, however, that he transferred the next year to the Baptist Bible College near Springfield, Missouri.

The turning point in his life came after graduation, when a pastor in Kansas City asked him to deliver a sermon while the pastor was out of town. Falwell nervously accepted but in the end felt at home at the pulpit.

"That Sunday, God used my sermon to bring nineteen souls to Christ," he recalled. "One of the converts was an elderly lady who . . . had heard many great preachers through the years, but God allowed this young novice the privilege of leading her to salvation. I have never doubted since that God called me to be a pastor."

Falwell was ordained at 22 and returned to Lynchburg, where he founded the Thomas Road Baptist Church. In 1968, he began broadcasting his Sunday sermons on TV and radio and launched his famous *Old Time Gospel Hour* program.

Throughout his career he has outraged Christians and non-Christians alike with his various political battles, including his libel suit against pornographer Larry Flynt* and his overtly sexist decree that all "good Christians" should have opposed the nomination of Sandra Day O'Connor** to the Supreme Court.

*See Larry Flynt, page 40.
**See Sandra Day O'Connor, page 109.

A Television Event

Philo Farnsworth turned 22 on August 19, 1928.

The man who invented the electric television at age 21 made a critical mistake at age 22 that cost him a lifetime of fame and fortune.

Philo Farnsworth grew up in Indian Springs, Utah, and was fascinated from an early age with electricity. He told his high school chemistry teacher he had an idea of how to send images electronically, involving an empty jar and a magnetically deflected beam of electrons. Perplexed, his teacher said he didn't see why it wouldn't work.

The idea of television wasn't new; the term itself was coined at the 1900 World's Fair in Paris. But the current technology was based on an electromechanical system, full of spinning disks, lenses, and filters, which transferred little more than globs of light.

At age 21, Farnsworth opened his own laboratory in Los Angeles and filed his first patent for an electric television. After creating a rudimentary prototype, he sought investors to fund the development of what he called an "image dissector," a forerunner of the cathode-ray tube. One prominent financier showed some interest. Farnsworth gave the man a demonstration and chose a symbolic image to transmit to his prototype television: a dollar sign. "This is something a banker will understand," Farnsworth said. The financier agreed to fund his work.

Two weeks after his 22nd birthday, Farnsworth made his big breakthrough. He announced to the press that his new image dissector would finally make electronic television possible. The *San Francisco Chronicle* splashed Farnsworth's picture on the front page, praised his "revolutionary" television system, and described his image dissector as "an ordinary quart jar that a housewife uses to preserve fruit."

While the young man enjoyed his success and plotted further

developments, media giant RCA was frustrated with its own effort to build an electronic television. Executives learned that Farnsworth welcomed visits from other inventors, so they sent their top television expert, Vladimir Zworykin, to see the young inventor.

According to many reports, Zworykin took obvious advantage of the 22-year-old's hospitality and spent three days poring over the inventions at Farnsworth's lab. When Farnsworth showed him his image dissector, Zworykin expressed admiration, and several witnesses heard him say, "This is a beautiful instrument. I wish I'd invented it."

Farnsworth's openness proved to be his downfall.

Zworykin returned to RCA and developed his own electronic television. While Farnsworth was still raising money to mass-produce his television, RCA launched a massive marketing campaign claiming it had invented the electric television. Although Farnsworth filed a series of patent-violation lawsuits against RCA —and eventually won after years of costly courtroom battles—the damage was done. RCA beat him to the market and temporarily rewrote history in the process.

Although all modern televisions descend directly from Farnsworth's design, he was never able to succeed financially on his invention. Few people today even know his name.

Legend of Zelda

F. Scott Fitzgerald turned 22 on September 24, 1918.

If F. Scott Fitzgerald didn't declare his love to a gorgeous young Southern belle right around his 22nd birthday, the Jazz Age may never have had its king and queen.

Long before Kurt and Courtney, and Sid and Nancy, there was Scott and Zelda—the hard-partying, self-destructive, and ultimately tragic icons of the Roaring Twenties. Their marriage made history, but their courtship put Fitzgerald through one of the toughest periods of his life, age 22—a year fraught with misery, rejection, and finally euphoria.

The St. Paul, Minnesota, native dropped out of Princeton with bad grades in 1917 and joined the Army. Believing he was destined to die in the Great War, Fitzgerald hastily wrote a semiautobiographical novel called *The Romantic Egoist,* during basic training. He submitted it to Charles Scribner's Sons. The publisher rejected it but praised its originality and encouraged the young writer to revise it.

Fitzgerald was transferred to Camp Sheridan, near Montgomery, Alabama. In the summer of 1918, he went to a dance at the Montgomery Country Club, where he met and fell in love with a beautiful 18-year-old debutant named Zelda Sayre. Fitzgerald became infatuated with her and in September pledged his love and asked for her hand in marriage. She accepted, and the two made the most of their time before he would be shipped out to Europe.

Two months later, however, Germany surrendered and Fitzgerald was never deployed. With a future wide open, he turned all of his energy on rewriting his novel. Zelda's father was a reputed Alabama Supreme Court judge, and Fitzgerald wanted to become an established author—with an acceptable income—before he married the young Southern belle. He finally sent his revised novel to Scribner's in January 1919. It was rejected again.

With his prospects as a novelist fading, Fitzgerald decided to make himself a worthy husband in a more old-fashioned way:* He moved to New York and got a job in advertising. But his salary was paltry, and Zelda was growing impatient. By June, their long-distance relationship broke under the strain and Zelda called off the engagement.

Distraught, Fitzgerald quit his job and returned to live with his parents in St. Paul. He locked himself in a studio and wrote for three months. Just before his 23rd birthday, Fitzgerald submitted the novel for a third time to Scribner's, this time with the title *This Side of Paradise*. The publisher accepted it.

Fitzgerald was elated and his artistic ambitions were revitalized. While waiting for the book to come out, he started writing short stories for magazines to make money. He also contacted Zelda and told her the news. By the time his debut novel was released, he had earned a reputation as a promising young writer. He also had money in the bank.

In March 1920, one week after his book came out, Scott and Zelda were married in the rectory at St. Patrick's Cathedral in New York. Fitzgerald went on to write several acclaimed short stories and novels, including *The Great Gatsby*** and *Tender Is the Night*.

*See Stephen Hawking, page 55, and Howard Stern, page 145.
**See Andy Kaufman, page 77.

Infidelity and Electroshock

Larry Flynt turned 22 on November 1, 1964.

At 22, Larry Flynt came to a conclusion that steered the rest of his life: "I decided I would never be faithful to any woman, ever again."

The future hard-core pornographer and First Amendment crusader grew up in Magoffin County, Kentucky, one of the poorest regions in the country. He longed for an education that would deliver him from poverty and free him from his Kentucky drawl.

Using a fake ID he joined the Army at age 15, with the hope of becoming an officer. But he was discharged after one year for failing his tests. He joined the Navy next, and served as a radio operator aboard the *USS Enterprise,* where he passed a high school equivalency exam.

In his early 20s, Flynt seemed eager to settle down and find a wife. He fell for a young woman, married her in a matter of days, but divorced her in a matter of weeks. Then, shortly after his 22nd birthday, he met and married the woman of his dreams.

"Peggy is the best thing that ever happened to me, because I was so very much in love with her," he said. "And then I got my heart ripped out." Soon after their wedding, Peggy became pregnant with another man's child while Flynt was away in the Navy. When he returned home and learned of the affair, he flew into a rage. The couple finally worked things out, and Flynt agreed to adopt the child.

Discharged from the military, Flynt returned to Dayton, Ohio, and was washing dishes and working at a factory to make ends meet. Peggy gave birth to Flynt's first daughter, Tonya, in 1965. Soon, though, the marriage started falling apart. Flynt accused Peggy of sleeping around again. "Peggy had no f—ing shame. No guilt," Flynt later said. "I was smart enough to take a lesson. I decided I would never be faithful to any woman, ever again."

One night, Flynt flew into a frenzy, grabbed a handgun, and fired shots over his wife's head. She fell down a staircase, and after he fled the scene, Flynt crashed his car into a tree. Police arrested him and he was sent to a psychiatric facility, where he received electroshock therapy that not only induced periods of amnesia, but also, some say, permanently changed his personality.

When he was released, Flynt and Peggy divorced, and the 22-year-old took all of his money and bought a tavern in Dayton, which he turned into a strip club. Targeting factory workers on their way home from work, Flynt's nude bar was an immediate success. By the time he was 25, he had expanded his operation and opened similar topless bars, which he named "Hustler Clubs," in Columbus, Cleveland, Akron, and Toledo. "I sensed that raw sex was what men wanted," Flynt once said. "And I was right."

In 1974, he launched *Hustler,* a hard-core porn magazine whose graphic photos and provocative content pushed the boundaries of free speech. Over the years, Flynt drew the ire of numerous religious leaders, including the Reverend Jerry Falwell,* who sued him for libel in 1983—a landmark case that went all the way to the Supreme Court.

*See Jerry Falwell, page 35.

Bathroom Break

Harrison Ford turned 22 on July 13, 1964.

One of the most popular action stars in history owes his success to a fateful trip to the men's room when he was 22 years old.

After dropping out of Ripon College in Wisconsin, where he'd majored in philosophy, Ford and his new wife, Mary Marquardt, packed up and moved to Los Angeles. The self-described "late bloomer" decided he'd try his luck as an actor—mostly because he'd enjoyed a few drama classes in college and couldn't think of anything else to do.

He landed a role in a summer stock production of *John Brown's Body* in Laguna Beach but attracted little notice. When an acquaintance offered to get him an appointment with the casting director at Columbia Pictures, he jumped at the chance. "I walked in, and they said, 'How tall are you, what do you weigh, do you speak any foreign languages, can you ride a horse?'" Ford recalled. He said the meeting ended with, "Okay, kid, thanks a lot, if we find anything we'll let you know."

Ford figured he'd flopped the interview and would never get a call. Nature called, though, and on his way out, he made a stop at the men's room. Afterward, he was looking for the elevator and ran into the casting director's assistant. The man offered him a $150-a-week contract, only because, Ford said, he needed one more person and Ford happened to be standing there. "I always knew right from the beginning that if I had gone down the elevator instead of going to take a pee, it wouldn't have been worth chasing me down the street."

That spring, at age 22, he was given a bit part in his first movie, *Dead Heat on a Merry-Go-Round,* in which he played a bellhop. His only line in the film may have foreshadowed his future role as a swashbuckling archaeologist: "Paging Mr. Jones, paging Mr. Jones."

Ford got bit parts in several other forgettable movies throughout the 1960s and had to work as a carpenter to pay the bills. His small role in 1973's *American Graffiti,* which was a surprise hit, finally cemented his acting career and established his relationship with George Lucas—who tapped Ford to play Han Solo in his *Star Wars* series a few years later.

On a Dare

Jamie Foxx turned 22 on December 13, 1989.

When Jamie Foxx was 22, his girlfriend dared him to perform during an open-mic night at a comedy club in Los Angeles. He accepted, and his impromptu impersonations not only delighted the crowd, but also marked a pivotal moment in his life.

Born Eric Bishop in Terrell, Texas, he had grown up singing in church choirs and aspiring to be a classical pianist.* He even won a music scholarship to United States International University in San Diego, where he met child prodigies from around the globe.

But after his fateful night at the comedy club, Bishop decided to give stand-up comedy a try. He said he adopted the androgynous stage name Jamie Foxx because many comedy clubs preferred female performers, and he wanted his name to stand out to the manager looking over the list.

Foxx performed all across California throughout his 22nd year and eventually won the Bay Area Black Comedy Competition. The achievement not only boosted his confidence, but also got him notice from one of comedy's hottest up-and-comers: Keenan Ivory Wayans. Wayans recruited Foxx for his hit TV show *In Living Color,* where numerous comics were already making a name for themselves, including Jim Carrey, David Alan Grier, and, of course, the Wayans brothers.

Foxx fit right in as a performer and writer of cutting-edge comedy sketches, and four years later was given his own comedy program, *The Jamie Foxx Show.*

*See Ansel Adams, page 1, and Condoleezza Rice, page 119.

"The Whole World Just Went Kablooey"

Jerry Garcia turned 22 on August 1, 1964.

Although Jerry Garcia's life in music began when he was a child, fate put him on the road to fame at age 22. Throughout 1964 and 1965, Garcia started meeting the people, doing the drugs, and creating the sound that led to the birth of the Grateful Dead, one of the most celebrated and influential bands of all time.

Musical instruments were omnipresent in Garcia's childhood home in San Francisco. His father was a jazz musician who played clarinet and saxophone; his mother played piano and sang. But tragedy hit Garcia early: He lost half of his right middle finger while chopping wood at age 4. Then, at age 5, he watched his father drown during a family vacation.

During his teenage years, Garcia couldn't cope with his high school regimen and wanted to escape his home life. He dropped out of school and joined the Army when he was 17. He quickly realized, however, that he also didn't belong in the military. After eight AWOL citations and two courts-martial, he was discharged.

Homeless, Garcia migrated to East Palo Alto, where he hung out at coffee shops around Stanford University and befriended Robert Hunter, a poet who would later write lyrics for the Grateful Dead. He also taught guitar lessons at a local record store to make money.

In early 1963, Garcia began playing folk songs at small venues with singer Sarah Ruppenthal, a woman he eventually got pregnant and married. Garcia tried to live a "straight life" as a husband and father but continued to pour his energy into music. He realized, however, he couldn't do it alone. "I got into old-time country music, old-time string band music," he said. "And in order to play string band music you have to have a band, you can't play

45

it by yourself."

Garcia joined Mother McCree's Uptown Jug Champions, a popular local bluegrass and folk band where he met guitarist Bob Weir and keyboardist Ron "Pigpen" McKernan. The three became friends, and after Garcia's 22nd birthday, they formed their own band, the Warlocks, with drummer Bill Kreutzmann, and, later, bassist Phil Lesh.

Gigs were hard to find. McKernan wanted the group to go electric, but it wasn't until Garcia saw the Beatles' movie *A Hard Day's Night** that he decided the band should plug in. "All of a sudden there were the Beatles," he explained. "You know, *Hard Day's Night,* wow. I thought, 'Hey, great, that really looks like fun.'"

But perhaps the most pivotal moment in Garcia's musical development came when he first tried acid,** at 22. "Along came LSD, and that was the end of the whole world. The whole world just went kablooey. Suddenly I realized that my little attempt at having a straight life was really a fiction and just wasn't going to work out," he said, referring to his marriage. "It was the same with my wife. . . . It freed us to be able to live our lives rather than having to live out an unfortunate social circumstance."

The acid trips also changed the music. The band started playing in the style it would become famous for: Long, energetic, free-form jams with folksy melodies and evocative lyrics.

The Warlocks debuted in July 1965, and the show was a success. Soon the group became the house band for Ken Kesey's Acid Tests—the underground parties where the famous novelist gave out LSD (before it was outlawed) and studied the reactions people had. The Warlocks became synonymous with the burgeoning psychedelic scene and started drawing larger crowds.

Not long after his 23rd birthday, Garcia learned that the name "the Warlocks" was already being used by another group. The band needed a new moniker. Garcia picked up an *Oxford Dictionary* at

Phil Lesh's house and opened it randomly. He landed on a page that contained a short Egyptian prayer. The first thing he saw were the two words *Grateful Dead.*

*See Ringo Starr, page 142.
**See Robert Crumb, page 31.

Bad Advice

Jennifer Garner turned 22 on April 17, 1994.

Not long after her 22nd birthday, Jennifer Garner approached a veteran stage actress for professional advice. The woman told her to hang up her acting dreams and become a paralegal—she would be happier and she would make more money.

The exchange only fueled Garner's desire to break into show business, and a few months later, she landed an understudy role on Broadway.

Garner had moved to New York after graduating from Denison University in Granville, Ohio, where she started off as a chemical engineering major but switched to drama. With no contacts in the city, Garner went to dozens of cattle-call auditions for both film and stage work, and waited tables at the famous Isabella's restaurant on the Upper West Side.

She finally got her break in 1994, when she was cast as an understudy in a production of *A Month in the Country*—which coincidentally starred Ron Rifkin, who would play her evil boss, Arvin Sloane, in the hit TV show *Alias* seven years later.

When the play ended, Garner decided to move to Los Angeles and focus on television. She won her first major role just before she turned 23, playing Melissa Gilbert's daughter in the miniseries *Zoya,* based on the book by Danielle Steel. The deal led to two other Hallmark Hall of Fame movies, which in turn got her a recurring role on the popular TV show *Felicity.*

Sketchy Business

Theodor "Dr. Seuss" Geisel turned 22 on March 2, 1926.

Doodling instead of taking notes at Oxford cost Theodor Geisel the chance to succeed at the esteemed university. But it also spurred him to fall in love, change his career ambitions, and permanently alter the course of his life.

Growing up in Springfield, Massachusetts, Geisel loved to draw and showed an early penchant for rendering ridiculous characters in absurd situations. He was a below-average student throughout high school, but his father was a prominent brewer and used his connections to get him into Dartmouth, where he majored in English literature.

Geisel got involved in the student humor magazine, *Jack-O-Lantern,* where he eventually became editor and published some of his first cartoons. When he was caught drunk on bootleg gin during Prohibition, administrators punished him by banning his work in the magazine. The move only prompted Geisel to publish under a pseudonym, and he started signing his cartoons with his mother's maiden name: Seuss.

After graduation, Geisel had no real ambitions, so he decided to become an English professor. He enrolled at Oxford, but within weeks was bored and distracted, doodling constantly in class. One of his classmates, Helen Marion Palmer, noticed his sketches and introduced herself. "That's a very fine flying cow," she told him. "What you really want to do is draw." Thus, Geisel, at age 22, met the woman he would marry and found the career he would pursue.

He quit Oxford that summer—later adding the "Dr." to "Seuss" to indicate the doctorate he never got—toured Europe, and started sending countless illustrations to New York with the hope of getting published. His first success was the *Saturday Evening Post,** which bought a cartoon for $25.

Spurred by that success, Geisel moved to New York and married Palmer. He landed his first full-time illustrator job at *Judge* magazine, where his work eventually earned him advertising jobs that sustained him through the Depression.

In 1937, the man who once said "adults are obsolete children" published his first of many beloved children's books, *And to Think That I Saw It on Mulberry Street.*

*See Norman Rockwell, page 122.

Change of Scenery

Jane Goodall turned 22 on April 3, 1956.

World-famous chimpanzee expert Jane Goodall once said, "Every individual matters. Every individual has a role to play. Every individual makes a difference."

No one was more pivotal to Goodall's career than one of her long-lost childhood friends, from whom she received an unexpected and life-changing letter a few weeks after her 22nd birthday.

Goodall grew up in a working-class family in London and from an early age was fascinated by exotic animals. Once at Christmas, she received *The Story of Dr. Dolittle,* the famous book about a doctor who travels across Africa talking to animals. The story gave the young girl a new vision for her life. "I had this dream of going to Africa," Goodall wrote. "I wanted to talk to the animals like Dr. Dolittle."

When she graduated high school, however, the family was too poor to send her to college, let alone Africa. Goodall's mother encouraged her to train as a secretary, because, she said, "secretaries could get jobs anywhere in the world." Goodall took the advice and enrolled in Queen's Secretarial College in South Kensington.

"What about my dream of Africa? Had I forgotten it? Absolutely not . . . I continued to read books about animals, especially African animals," Goodall remembered. "Always I was waiting for my lucky break. When that lucky break finally came, I was ready."

That break came in the mail. Goodall received a letter from her old school friend Marie-Claude Mange, whose parents had just bought a farm in Kenya and who wanted to know if Goodall would like to visit. Goodall was elated. She wrote back saying she would come as soon as she had the money. She quit her secretary job and waited tables for ten months, working double shifts and stashing away her tips.

In March 1957, Goodall finally had enough money for a ticket aboard the passenger liner *Kenya Castle*. Goodall set foot in Africa one day before her 23rd birthday. She met her friend and spent several weeks touring the country and seeing a slew of wild animals. Then another lucky break came her way.

She met Dr. Louis Leakey, a prominent paleontologist who was embarking on a fossil-finding expedition and was looking for a secretary. Goodall mentioned her clerical skills and he hired her on the spot.

After that expedition, Leakey was so impressed with Goodall's thirst for zoological knowledge that he asked her if she would be interested in studying a group of wild chimpanzees he'd come across in Tanzania. For Goodall, it was the opportunity of a lifetime.

In 1960, Jane Goodall set up a research camp in Tanzania and launched an exhaustive forty-year study of chimpanzees, which became a milestone in the field. Her meticulous work has earned her numerous honors and worldwide recognition.

California Dreamin'

Woody Guthrie turned 22 on July 14, 1934.

"California is a garden of Eden," Woody Guthrie once sang. "But believe it or not, you won't find it so hot if you ain't got the do re mi." The song sums up the turning point of his life at age 22.

Like thousands of other "Okies," Woody and the Guthrie family packed their bags and migrated to California to look for work after the great dust storms of the 1930s. A few years earlier, the young man from Okemah, Oklahoma, had moved to the Texas panhandle, got married, and had three children. But by 22, his world was upside down and he decided to move to Los Angeles, where his cousin Jack Guthrie was working in the entertainment business.

During the slow trip westward, Guthrie witnessed firsthand the misery and suffering of thousands of migrant workers, later detailed in John Steinbeck's *The Grapes of Wrath.* He'd been playing the guitar and harmonica since his teens, and during the trip west started writing songs that described the torment around him. He typed up his lyrics into a songbook he called *Alonzo M. Zilch's Own Collection of Original Songs and Ballads.*

By most accounts, Guthrie landed in Los Angeles* a few months before his 23rd birthday. He started performing his songs at workers' rallies and other political gatherings and gained a reputation as a spokesman for the alienated masses. Guthrie, who once said, "If you play more than two chords, you're showing off," became a local star and regular performer on KFVD radio.

He soon met fellow musician Cisco Houston, who was to become a lifelong friend, and the pair began performing folk music and protest songs that resonated across the country. In 1939, Guthrie rode the rails to New York, where he formally recorded many of his songs for the Library of Congress and where he also wrote his signature piece, "This Land Is Your Land."

*See Matt Drudge, page 33, and Brad Pitt, page 114.

Young and Restless

David Hasselhoff turned 22 on July 17, 1974.

The man famous around the world for TV's *Knight Rider* and *Baywatch**—and in Germany for his singing career—got his big break in show business fresh out of college.

David Hasselhoff knew early he wanted to be an actor, but he always imagined himself in musicals.** The Baltimore native persuaded his parents to sign him up for singing and dancing lessons at age 7. By the time he was a teenager, "the Hoff," as he was known, was starring in numerous high school productions.

While studying at the California Institute of the Arts in Valencia, Hasselhoff prepared for a career in musical theater, but after graduation he changed his mind and started auditioning for TV shows. The pivotal moment came at age 22, when he tried out for a role on the soap opera *The Young and the Restless.*

Hasselhoff landed the part of the socially conscious Dr. William "Snapper" Foster Jr. and became a well-known face in households across the country over the next six years. His work on the daytime soap led to a starring role as Michael Knight on the hit show *Knight Rider* in the 1980s.

Hasselhoff finally fulfilled his childhood dream of being a singer when he released his debut album *Night Rocker* in 1985. He became a sensation in Germany, where he released ten albums in the following decade.

*See Pamela Anderson, page 6.
**See Zadie Smith, page 138.

Death Sentence

Stephen Hawking turned 22 on January 8, 1964.

Stephen Hawking was supposed to be dying, but at age 22 he was acting like he'd just been reborn. When most young adults faced broad futures full of possibilities, Hawking was handed a death sentence. Doctors diagnosed him with Lou Gehrig's disease just after his 21st birthday. It was advancing rapidly, and they said he probably wouldn't live past 25. After sinking into a deep depression, however, the young physicist found renewed strength in an unexpected place.

Born in Oxford, England, in 1942, Hawking was a highly intelligent child but socially awkward. He wanted to study mathematics, but his father, a noted medical researcher, urged him to enter medicine. By way of compromise, Hawking decided to enter the natural sciences and studied physics at Oxford, his father's alma mater. After graduating in just three years, the young scientist decided to pursue a Ph.D. in cosmology at Cambridge.

Throughout 1962, however, Hawking noticed he was becoming clumsy, had trouble tying his shoes, and sometimes had difficulty speaking. During the Christmas holiday, his mother persuaded him to see a doctor. A series of tests concluded with the staggering diagnosis of advanced motor neuron disease (MND). His excitement about studying cosmology, his plans for the future, became meaningless.

Hawking sank into a depression and holed up in his college room. "I felt somewhat of a tragic character. I took to listening to Wagner," he once said. "I regarded Wagner as music that was dark enough for my mood."

He also recalled wishing he'd be given a second chance. "Before my condition had been diagnosed, I had been very bored with life. There had not seemed to be anything worth doing.

But shortly after I came out of the hospital I dreamt that I was going to be executed. I suddenly realized that there were a lot of worthwhile things I could do, if I were reprieved."

Though reprieve from his crippling disease seemed unlikely, Hawking found inspiration in an area in which he'd never had much luck: romance. He fell in love with Jane Wilde, a young woman he met through a family friend. And she fell for Hawking, vowing to take care of him as his condition deteriorated. When he proposed marriage, she happily accepted. "The engagement changed my life," Hawking later said. "It gave me something to live for."

Once consumed by his impending death, Hawking's thoughts now shifted to his fiancée. He wanted to marry her before he died, but social convention required him to be gainfully employed.* To get married, he needed a job; to get a job, he needed a doctorate; to get a doctorate meant he had to get back to work. At 22, Hawking decided to put his depression behind him. "One has to be grown up enough to realize that life is not fair. You just have to do the best you can in the situation you are in," Hawking later said. "I therefore started working for the first time in my life. To my surprise I found I liked it."

He also set his sights extremely high: His thesis was to apply Roger's singularity theory to the entire universe. He amazed his professors and colleagues with his innovative work.

In 1965, Hawking published his thesis and was awarded a Ph.D. from Cambridge. The paper sparked admiration across the world of cosmology and secured Hawking's professional career. Immediately after he got his Ph.D., he landed a job. And immediately after that, he married Jane Wilde.

The year was 1965, and the time period he'd been given to live was expired. As his condition worsened, Hawking continued his work with his wife's help. He decided to live day by day and enjoy whatever time he had left. That was forty years ago, and the young scientist given a death sentence in his early 20s has since then furthered the work of Einstein and expanded humanity's understanding of the universe.

See F. Scott Fitzgerald, page 38, and Howard Stern, page 145.

Some Free Advice

Ernest Hemingway turned 22 on July 21, 1921.

Ernest Hemingway knew when to listen. That is how, at age 22, he made the one decision that, more than any other, put him on the road toward becoming an icon in American literature.

After World War I, the aspiring author moved to Chicago and rented an apartment near the home of Sherwood Anderson, the famous novelist who had a reputation for his willingness to help young writers. Hemingway had landed regular freelance assignments at the *Toronto Star,* but he wanted to improve his fiction writing. He introduced himself to Anderson. The two instantly became friends and saw each other almost daily for two years.

Anderson learned how Hemingway had wanted to be a writer since he was in high school in Oak Park, Illinois. Instead of going to college, he got a job as a cub reporter for the *Kansas City Star.* When he was old enough, Hemingway tried to enlist in the Army but was denied because of poor vision. He found an alternative way to help the war effort: He signed up as a volunteer ambulance driver for the Red Cross.

During their many long walks and late-night meals together, Anderson and Hemingway shared their thoughts and stories. Anderson told tales of his own childhood and early efforts in writing. He also offered honest, sometimes brutal, critiques of Hemingway's work. The young writer appreciated it and took endless notes. "I didn't know how to write until I met Sherwood Anderson," Hemingway once said.

But of all the things he got from the experienced writer, it was a single piece of advice Anderson gave him after his 22nd birthday that changed everything.

Hemingway had just married his first wife, Hadley Richardson, and the two were deciding where to live. Anderson encouraged him to move to Paris. He said a new generation of artists, poets, and writers was gathering there. He told Hemingway he should be part of it. The 22-year-old thought it over and took the advice.

He arrived in Paris on December 8, 1921, with letters of introduction from Anderson to Ezra Pound and Gertrude Stein. They were his tickets into the heart of an expatriate enclave soon to be known as the Lost Generation. Through Pound and Stein, Hemingway met several artists who would help him hone his writing style, including F. Scott Fitzgerald,* James Joyce, John Dos Passos, and Ford Maddox Ford. Of all those, Fitzgerald helped him the most by convincing his publisher, Scribner's, to look at Hemingway's work.

In addition to the incredible contacts he made, Hemingway also found a world of material to write about in Paris. His first novel, *The Sun Also Rises,* taps into that expatriate scene, and one of his last works, *A Moveable Feast,* celebrates it: "If you are lucky enough to have lived in Paris as a young man, then wherever you go for the rest of your life it stays with you, for Paris is a moveable feast."

*See F. Scott Fitzgerald, page 38.

French Connection

Audrey Hepburn turned 22 on May 4, 1951.

A chance encounter with a world-famous author transformed 22-year-old Audrey Hepburn from a struggling ballet dancer in London to an acclaimed actress on Broadway.

Born in England and raised in Holland, Hepburn witnessed the atrocities committed by the Nazis during World War II. Her family lost everything when the Germans invaded in 1940, and Hepburn at age 11 started helping the Resistance by delivering secret messages and documents she hid in her shoes. She also started dancing in underground performances and dreamed of becoming a ballet star as an escape from the misery around her.

After the war, she moved to London with her mother and pursued ballet full-time. Although she applied herself rigorously, she eventually realized that her odds of success were extremely small, that her talents weren't sufficient in such a highly competitive field. While auditioning for ballet troupes, she decided also to start trying out for musicals in London. After getting cast in a bit part in the musical *High Button Shoes,* she landed walk-on roles in several European films. One of those jobs led her to the luckiest day of her life.

Not long after her 22nd birthday, Hepburn traveled to the French Riviera, where she had landed a tiny part in the film *Nous Irons à Monte Carlo.* While strolling across a hotel lobby with members of the film crew, Hepburn was spotted by the renowned French author Colette. In Hepburn's natural beauty and grace, Colette saw the walking embodiment of the main character of her novel *Gigi.* She approached the young dancer and insisted that she star in the Broadway musical version. Hepburn jumped at the opportunity.

She flew to New York and gave a formal audition for the show. Although the director found her reading disappointing, Hepburn got the lead role at Colette's insistence. Hepburn's biggest asset was her elegance, her biggest liability her voice. She worked tirelessly with a vocal coach all the way up to opening night.

The show premiered on November 24, 1951, and though it got low marks overall, critics across the board praised Hepburn's performance. She even won a Theatre World Award.

She became an instant star, and Hollywood came clamoring. After her six-month run on Broadway, she was cast opposite Gregory Peck in the 1953 film *Roman Holiday,* for which she won an Academy Award for Best Actress. She went on to star in dozens of classics, including *Funny Face, Breakfast at Tiffany's,* and *My Fair Lady.*

Alien Obsession

J. Edgar Hoover turned 22 on January 1, 1917.

The chief of the FBI for almost a half century was notorious for his obsession with rooting out radicals and subversives—an obsession that began when he was 22 years old.

John Edgar Hoover worked his way through law school at George Washington University by serving as a messenger in the Library of Congress. He felt empowered by his role as an information bearer and when he graduated in the spring of 1917 decided he wanted to work in intelligence. He avoided military service in World War I by persuading his uncle, a prominent judge, to call in a favor at the Justice Department. His uncle complied, and the 22-year-old Hoover was appointed a special agent at the Bureau of Investigation, the forerunner of the FBI.

He was made an assistant in the foreign registration section, or Alien Enemy Bureau, where he monitored foreign radicals living in the United States who were suspected of subversive behavior. Hoover became renowned for his diligence: He kept in-depth statistics and lengthy files on the people he monitored. He became consumed to the point of paranoia in his hunt for communists and other political radicals he believed were trying to take down the country from the inside.

His first job out of college set the pattern for his life: He became a crusader against subversion in all forms. And he was quickly rewarded for his work.

In 1919, Hoover was named special assistant to the U.S. attorney general and played a key role in the infamous Palmer Raid of November 7, in which more than 10,000 suspected anarchists and communists were arrested on the second anniversary of the Russian Revolution.

Five years later, President Calvin Coolidge appointed Hoover the director of the FBI, a post he held until his death in 1972.

The Hard Sell

Wayne Huizenga turned 22 on December 29, 1959.

The tough-as-nails entrepreneur who built Blockbuster Video and Waste Management into Fortune 500 companies and who owns the Miami Dolphins (of the N.F.L.) and the Florida Panthers (of the N.H.L.) learned a life-changing lesson at 22 while making rounds as a door-to-door salesman—a lesson that also put him in court on assault charges.

H. Wayne Huizenga watched his family's fortune crumble while growing up in Fort Lauderdale. He loafed for five years after high school—taking a series of low-paying jobs, enrolling briefly in college, and serving a stint in the Army Reserve—and upon returning to south Florida took a job at a trash-hauling service, Pompano Carting. He was hired to knock on doors and get people to switch garbage companies.

Huizenga was an extremely aggressive pitchman. A few months before his 23rd birthday, he refused to take no for an answer from homeowner Thomas Millwood. He not only refused to leave the man's house, but attacked Millwood in a fit of anger, according to a civil lawsuit.

Millwood, who claimed the altercation left him with a ripped shirt and broken sunglasses, sued Huizenga. He said the most painful part of the attack was the "permanent injury to the testicles and genital area as a result of grabbing and twisting by the defendant."

Huizenga denied the charges in court, but a jury found in Millwood's favor and awarded him $1,000 in damages. The bizarre attack marked a major turning point in the 22-year-old's life: He learned the art of the hard sell without the violence. A year later, he bought a broken-down garbage truck and launched his own company, Waste Management, which over the next two decades he built into a multibillion-dollar enterprise.

Change of Plans

Curtis "50 Cent" Jackson turned 22 on July 6, 1998.

Curtis Jackson, the rapper better known as 50 Cent, once told an interviewer that his hip-hop name is "a metaphor for change."

Born and raised on the south side of Jamaica, Queens, where his mother was murdered when he was 8, where his father abandoned him, and where he started dealing crack in grade school, 50 Cent had plenty of reasons to seek a change in life. He set out to reinvent himself in his late teens and wound up making a decision at 22 that changed everything.

By the time he was in high school, 50 Cent was running a widespread crack operation that brought him more than $5,000 a day—as well as two felony drug convictions and stints in juvenile detention. "Life is cheap in those places," he once said. "You can have someone killed for $5,000."

As he got older, he tried to find ways to get out of dealing. He had always aspired to be a boxer, but when he started drawing attention as a rapper at parties, his dreams shifted to a career in hip-hop. In 1996, a friend introduced him to Jam Master Jay, cofounder of the seminal rap group Run-DMC, who took 50 Cent under his wing. "Jay taught me about bars, Jay taught me how to write hooks," 50 Cent recalled, "and Jay taught me how to write and make rap records. He made me want to really rap and do this."

Eager to make a name for himself, 50 Cent made a fateful choice when he was 22: Despite the advantages of being connected to Jam Master Jay, he decided to leave Jay's record label and started releasing his own tracks on underground mix tapes. "I worked the streets," he said. "The mix tapes are the entry level of hip-hop. So I saturated the streets, the black market."

The strategy paid off. 50 Cent built a reputation as an authentic street "gangsta," whose real-life crimes and gunfights made some mainstream hip-hop seem artificial. His name spread so fast that in 1999, he was approached by Track Masters, a hip-hop production team who saw a future in the rapper's raw power and incisive lyrics, and then signed by Columbia Records.

At age 22, 50 Cent locked himself in a recording studio in upstate New York for eighteen days and made his first professional recordings. Thirty-six songs came out of the session, and his debut album was later hailed as an instant classic by *Blaze* magazine.

That summer, Track Masters released the single "How to Rob," a satirical rhyme about how easily 50 Cent could steal from a pantheon of hip-hop personalities, including Jay-Z, Busta Rhymes, and Ja Rule. In one part, 50 Cent boasts that he'll kidnap Lil' Kim and demand ransom from Sean Combs.*

Though the recording put 50 Cent in the spotlight, many of the rappers taunted in the song weren't amused. Jay-Z, Big Pun, Sticky Fingaz, and Ghostface Killah all lashed out at the up-and-comer, and ultimately Columbia dropped 50 Cent before releasing his debut album. The song touched off so much ire within the hip-hop industry, in fact, that 50 Cent was twice attacked after the track was released. He was stabbed at a New York club in March 2000 and two months later was shot nine times outside his grandmother's house in Queens. He survived the assault but spent two weeks recovering in the hospital.

The shooting only helped speed 50 Cent's rise to fame. In 2002, Eminem signed him to a seven-figure contract on his Shady Records label, where 50 Cent went on to produce the album *Get Rich or Die Tryin'*, a phenomenal success.

*See Sean "Diddy" Combs, page 25.

Second Chance

"Shoeless Joe" Jackson turned 22 on July 16, 1911.

After an inauspicious start in the big leagues and an embarrassing trip back to the minors, one of the greatest players in the history of baseball made a dazzling comeback when he was 22 —and set a record that has stood for almost a century.

Joe Jackson grew up playing baseball in his hometown of Greenville, South Carolina, and not much else. He dropped out of school before learning to read or write and in between ball games pulled shifts at the mill where his father worked. He became a local legend on the diamond, and in 1908, a scout discovered him and signed him to the Philadelphia Athletics.

Life in the majors, and in the big city, was not much fun for the Southern boy. His teammates teased him mercilessly about his illiteracy and rural background; when they learned that he'd played an entire minor league game in his socks because his spikes had given him blisters, they called him "Shoeless Joe"—a nickname he hated.

He also put up awful stats during the very few games he actually played that season: He got only 6 hits out of 40 at-bats. Jackson was miserable and started not showing up for games. The owner finally traded him to the Cleveland franchise, where Jackson was sent back to the minors. Happy again, he started playing the way he used to.

In 1911, he got his second chance in the majors when the Cleveland Naps (later renamed the Indians) called him up. This time, he played spectacularly and in one season proved himself one of the greatest batters of all time. By the end of the year, Jackson had 233 hits and a batting average of .408—the only rookie in history to bat over .400.

The 22-year-old became a celebrity and enjoyed life in the spotlight, although he still had to deal with hecklers: Once, while he was at bat, a woman sitting near third base shouted, "Hey, Joe, how do you spell 'illiterate'?"

Unflustered, Jackson smashed a ball into the outfield, rounded the bases, and slid into third. As he stood up, he called out to her, "Hey, lady, how do you spell 'triple'?" In one interview, he said, "I ain't afraid to tell the world that it didn't take school stuff to help a fella play ball."

At 22, Jackson started down the path to becoming one of the greatest hitters of his era. His reputation suffered a devastating blow in 1920, however, when he and seven other players were accused of throwing the World Series of 1919 in what became known as the Black Sox scandal. Consequently, Jackson was banished for life from organized baseball and excluded from the Baseball Hall of Fame.

The Comeback Kid

Billy Joel turned 22 on May 9, 1971.

He enjoyed some success as a musician in his teens, but in his early 20s, Billy Joel suffered a spectacular failure. He was humiliated and suicidal, and decided there was nothing left to do but scrap everything and start over.

Joel grew up on Long Island playing piano and dreaming of being in a rock band. In high school, he joined his first band, the Echoes, a group that played British Invasion covers and drew respectable crowds. When the band's popularity took off, Joel dropped out of high school to pursue music full-time. The experience actually landed him his first professional recording work: He was recruited to play piano on the Shangri-Las' *Leader of the Pack* in 1964.

After playing two years with the Echoes, he left to join the Hassles, a bubble-gum pop group in which Joel started to write his own songs. The band released two albums back-to-back. But both were such commercial failures, the group disbanded months after the albums hit the shelves. Joel and Hassles drummer Jon Small, however, stuck together and formed an organ-percussion duo called Attila.

It was 1969, and Joel and Small wanted to tap into the burgeoning psychedelic* sound. Joel wired his organ with a range of special-effects pedals and pounded out loud formless tunes, while Small delivered irregular rhythms on a similarly rigged drum set. On the cover of their eponymous debut album, Joel and Small appear in barbarian costumes, presumably dressed as Huns. An interview is printed on the back in which Joel says he "sweats" only two things in life: perfecting his sound and the war in Southeast Asia.

Attila's first and only album was an overnight bomb. Years later, Joel disowned the work, calling it "psychedelic bullshit." The duo split up but with some emotional tangles: Joel had started an affair with Small's wife, Elizabeth, who soon left the drummer for the organist.

Bitterly disappointed and humiliated by Attila's failure, Joel sank into a depression and even tried to kill himself by drinking a bottle of furniture polish. After that, he decided to check into a hospital for psychiatric treatment. He eventually started working again, writing for a rock magazine and performing jingles for television commercials.

Joel made a fresh start in his musical career in 1971. He won a recording contract with a small producer in New York and released his first solo album, *Cold Spring Harbor,* in November. Although the LP garnered decent reviews, Joel was still unhappy with his efforts. He decided he needed a change.

At 22, Joel packed up and moved to Los Angeles. He landed a job at the Executive Room on Wilshire Boulevard. For six months, he played lounge piano and often delivered a little stand-up comedy between songs. "At the time I said I don't believe people do this for years and years and don't have much hope in getting beyond playing in a piano bar," Joel once said. "I said I got to write a song about this."

He wrote what would become his signature tune, "Piano Man," which won him a contract with Columbia Records and a 1973 critically acclaimed album of the same name. In 1985, his marriage to supermodel Christie Brinkley** made headlines. They were divorced in 1994.

*See David Bowie, page 14.
**See Christie Brinkley, page 17.

Spared from Death

Pope John Paul II turned 22 on May 18, 1942.

"At 20, I had already lost all the people I loved," Pope John Paul II once lamented. But at 22, he discovered "the true path" of his life and gave up everything to pursue it.

Born and raised in southern Poland, Karol Józef Wojtyla lost his mother when he was 9, his only brother when he was 12, and his father when he was 20. He also watched many of his closest friends get sent to concentration camps after the Nazis invaded his homeland in 1939.

The young poet, actor, and philosophy student was spared because he began working twelve hours a day in a limestone quarry in Kraków. In fact, he would become only the second pope in history who was once a manual laborer. "When I received orders to work the second and third shifts without rest," he later recalled, "the old workers came to me with a piece of bread and said, 'Eat, brainy fellow, you should not go hungry, you should survive. For your bright future is coming.'"

When the Nazis closed all universities and libraries, Wojtyla and his friends began staging underground performances in what they called the Rhapsodic Theater. Members of the secret group took considerable risks: Anyone caught with subversive literature was sent to a concentration camp.

An aspiring playwright who had already learned nine languages, Wojtyla poured his sorrow and anger into epic poems that were modeled after Greek tragedies. He wanted to fight fascism by creating "a theater that will be a church where the national spirit will burn." His dramatic poetry usually tapped biblical subjects and exhibited a range of styles, from his traditional blank-verse trilogy, *David, Job, and Jeremiah,* to his avant-garde play *Our God's Brother.*

In 1942, several members of the Rhapsodic Theater were

arrested and sent to Auschwitz, where they were later executed. "Sometimes I ask myself, 'So many people at my age were losing their lives, why not me?'" he once wrote. He decided he'd been spared for a reason.

Wojtyla had grown up respecting his father's devout Catholicism. After he turned 22, he surprised his friends by quitting the theater and devoting his life to the Church. Because Nazis were sentencing all priests to death, Wojtyla entered an underground seminary run by the archbishop of Kraków, Cardinal Sapieha, in October 1942. For more than two years, he led a double life: quarry worker by day, clandestine seminary student by night.

After the Nazis were defeated and Poland regained its independence, Wojtyla formally continued his studies. He was ordained to the priesthood on November 1, 1946.

In 1978, Wojtyla was elected pope, the first non-Italian pontiff in 450 years. He served until his death in 2005.

Struck a Blue Note

Norah Jones turned 22 on March 30, 2001.

Her debut album scored eight Grammy Awards, including album of the year, and made her an overnight celebrity. Recorded and released when she was 22 years old, *Come Away with Me* marked a major turning point in Norah Jones's life.

Jones dropped out of her jazz piano program at the University of North Texas and moved to New York in 1999 to try her luck as a performer. The daughter of renowned sitarist Ravi Shankar—who taught George Harrison the instrument—Jones grew up immersed in music and aspired to perform her own songs. At age 21, after arriving in Manhattan, she joined her first band, the funk-fusion group Wax Poetic. The band recorded a demo tape for legendary jazz label Blue Note, but it was Jones who captured the talent scouts' attention. She signed a recording contract and was brought into the studio just after her 22nd birthday.

Her initial recording sessions produced extremely guitar-heavy songs, which the executives thought drowned out Jones's "angelic" voice. They decided to scrap everything and start over. The label brought in a new producer, Arif Mardin, who emphasized Jones's singing on the next set of recordings. The resulting album was a magnificent blend of blues, folk, and jazz that would sell more than 18 million copies.

Jones herself was surprised by the debut album, especially considering she was 22 years old and had been playing professionally for less than a year. "I never thought I'd have a record like this," she once said. "I thought it would be at least five years before I'd reach that point. This is really the record I wanted to make."

You Can't Go Home Again

Janis Joplin turned 22 on January 19, 1965.

After living the rock-and-roll lifestyle for two years in San Francisco, drinking obscenely, sleeping around, and doing countless drugs, Janis Joplin decided she'd had enough. After her 22nd birthday, she returned to her small hometown in Texas, enrolled in college, got engaged, and tried to settle down to a suburban life. She thought she needed to be more "normal," but 22 turned out to be the most abnormal year of her exceptional—and short—life.

Joplin grew up in Port Arthur, Texas, listening to blues and singing in a church choir. In high school, her acne and overweight figure made her deeply insecure, and she sought companionship in a group of young beatniks. She gradually became the school rebel, wore outrageous clothes, drank whiskey, and cursed constantly. She also started singing at roadhouses, mostly doing imitations of her favorite blues singers: Odetta, Bessie Smith, and Leadbelly.

She enrolled at the University of Texas at Austin in 1962, where her counterculture attitudes drew some praise that she desperately craved, but also some vicious ridicule. Some frat boys nominated her for their "Ugliest Man on Campus" contest and ran her picture in the school newspaper. Joplin tried to laugh it off, but she was humiliated. She dropped out of college in 1963 and hitchhiked to San Francisco, where she hoped she would fit in with other beatniks and hippies on the Haight-Ashbury* scene.

She thrived in California. Landing singing gigs at coffeehouses around the Bay Area, Joplin finally met people who encouraged her and audiences who loved her. She mesmerized crowds with her incredible three-octave range, gravelly voice, and powerful blues style. She also started experimenting with drugs, and became addicted to methamphetamine. Friends worried as they watched her body transform. After two years, she weighed only eighty-eight pounds. Exhausted, depressed, and strung out, Joplin realized she was self-destructing. She decided she couldn't live this way. At age 22, she got on a bus and went back home to Texas.

Her parents greeted her with open arms and nursed her back to health. She went sober and started seeing a psychiatrist. She cut her hair, started wearing business suits, and enrolled in classes at Lamar Tech. She stopped singing and avoided parties. She even got engaged to a man named Peter DeBlanc, himself a recovering meth addict. She tried earnestly to live a regimented life. It didn't last long.

Just before her 23rd birthday, a friend in San Francisco called and encouraged her to audition for lead singer in a promising band called Big Brother and the Holding Company. Joplin weighed the two lifestyles before her: small-town and subdued versus big-city and boisterous. She chose the latter and packed her bags. She won the lead singer audition and signed her first major recording contract.

In 1967, she became a rock icon with "Piece of My Heart" and her electrifying performances at the Monterey Pop and Woodstock festivals. She died at 27 from a heroin overdose, two weeks after the death of fellow rock star Jimi Hendrix.

See Jerry Garcia, page 45, and Robert Crumb, page 31.

A Little Help from His Friend

Franz Kafka turned 22 on July 3, 1905.

Highly private, self-deprecating, and full of doubts, Franz Kafka possessed a literary genius that was nearly snuffed out by his mortal fear of being published. But at age 22, he argued with a certain young man about Nietzsche—an act that led to the creation and preservation of his now world-renowned work.

Kafka spent most of his life in Prague, where as a child he read constantly and aspired to be a writer. He composed poems and plays for his family to perform at birthday parties and when he was 16 started writing fiction. From the beginning, however, he exhibited a bizarre hatred of his own work. Almost as soon as he finished writing something, he destroyed it. The habit continued well into college.

A pragmatist, Kafka knew he couldn't rely on making a living as a writer. He pursued several fields in college—chemistry, philosophy, the humanities—before landing in what he considered the most versatile field of all: law. But he continued to write on the side, and after abandoning his first attempt at a novel in 1904, he began work on a short story that he wrestled with for five years, the aptly named "Description of a Struggle."

To break up all his legal studies, Kafka took a philosophy course on Schopenhauer a few months after his 22nd birthday. During one class, his young lecturer called Friedrich Nietzsche a fraud. Kafka objected. The two got into a debate that went on for hours after the class ended. The man was Max Brod, and he became one of the best friends Kafka ever had.

Brod was a self-proclaimed polymath—writer, poet, musician, philosopher, critic—and Kafka agreed to show him a draft of his short story. Brod read it and spotted Kafka's gift. He insisted Kafka publish it immediately, but the self-loathing writer resisted. The more Kafka questioned his abilities, the more Brod encouraged him. It was the first of a lifetime of such encounters.

Brod worked tirelessly to stop his friend from burning manuscripts and have him instead submit them for publication. Eventually, Kafka submitted "Description of a Struggle," and it was published. Thanks to the support of his friend, he continued to write regularly until he succumbed to tuberculosis at age 40.

While he was dying, Kafka instructed both his lover Dora Dymant and Brod to destroy all of his manuscripts. Dymant complied and burned every piece of his writing she had. Brod, however, ignored Kafka's demand and set about the task of editing and publishing every story in his possession, including *America, The Trial,* and *The Castle.*

Without Brod's denial of a deathbed request, the world may have lost some of the work of one of its most creative authors, whose morbid imagination and deep feelings of alienation, torment, and frustration with modern life fueled a new generation of writers.

Transcendental Comedy

Andy Kaufman turned 22 on January 17, 1971.

Before he became the world's ultimate anti-comedian, Andy Kaufman took two trips during his 22nd year that were pivotal to his success—one to Spain and one to his hometown of Roslyn, New York.

While working toward an associate's degree in applied science at Grahm Junior College in Boston, Kaufman discovered Transcendental Meditation,* the Eastern method of exploring one's consciousness that gained popularity in America in the 1960s. Kaufman found it a perfect tool to battle his intense stage fright. "I knew I had the potential to entertain, but I was too shy," he once said. "TM really brought the shyness out of me."

In the spring of 1971, with a diploma and no job plans, Kaufman decided to deepen his devotion to Transcendental Meditation. He journeyed to Majorca, Spain, and enrolled in an intense TM program that taught him to focus his thoughts one by one until he had arrived at the "source of his creative energy." Kaufman gained tremendous peace and clarity through meditation, and he practiced it the rest of his life.

Between seminars, he traveled through Europe, visited many cities, and honed some of the comic material he had performed on his college TV station. He returned to the United States more eager than ever to pursue stand-up.

Instead of staying in Boston, however, where he'd already made contacts in local clubs and TV stations, Kaufman moved home and tried to break into the comedy circuit on Long Island—a decision that proved pivotal. After numerous auditions, he landed a stand-up gig at a rock club called My Father's Place.

His early performances were like his later ones. He amused, angered, and often bored audiences with baffling acts. He would read *The Great Gatsby*** page by page or sing "100 Bottles of Beer on the Wall" in its entirety. His Elvis impersonations and Mighty Mouse lip-synching got laughs, but more often his audiences heckled or abandoned him.

His big break came a few months before his 23rd birthday. Budd Friedman, owner of the Improv in New York, stopped by the small club to scout out the local talent. "He had a company of players who were mostly waitresses or ex-waitresses," Friedman said. "He'd bring 'em up like somebody out of the audience and pick fights with them and slap them and pull their hair. People didn't quite get it."

But Friedman got it. He saw a promising originality in Kaufman and invited him to perform at the Improv. Kaufman's act got people talking, and he soon landed regular gigs all over New York and Los Angeles. The exposure got him an appearance on the inaugural broadcast of *Saturday Night Live* in 1975, which clinched his fame.

Kaufman went on to costar in the TV sitcom *Taxi* as Latka Gravas, a version of one of his oldest stand-up characters. He also became a wrestler, declared himself "Intergender Wrestling Champion of the World," and offered $1,000 to any woman who could pin him. Throughout his eccentric career, he never broke character, neither on stage nor off. Some people even thought his sudden death of lung cancer in 1984 was a hoax.

*See Howard Stern, page 145.
**See F. Scott Fitzgerald, page 38.

The Story of Her Life

Helen Keller turned 22 on June 27, 1902.

After overcoming her tremendous physical handicaps, Helen Keller set out to write her life's story at age 22—an effort that made her one of the most famous women in the world.

Born in Tuscumbia, Alabama, Keller was a typical, healthy baby girl until she came down with a severe fever when she was 19 months old. The illness led to an acute congestion of the brain, which left her blind, deaf, and unable to speak.

The traumatic loss of these senses deprived her of the ability to communicate or fully experience the world at a key developmental age, and she grew into a desperate, uncontrollable child. After contacting numerous agencies for help, her parents finally found the Perkins Institute for the Blind in Boston. The organization sent Anne Sullivan, a 20-year-old teacher, to meet with Keller. The event marked the beginning of a forty-nine year relationship.

Sullivan taught Keller the fundamentals of language, using the Tadoma method: making signs in Helen's hands, connecting those signs to real objects, building an alphabet and vocabulary, then touching each other's lips as they spoke, to learn the rhythm of language. The tutoring worked phenomenally well. "Suddenly I felt a misty consciousness as of something forgotten—a thrill of returning thought; and somehow the mystery of language was revealed to me," Keller wrote.

As her world opened up, Keller proved to be an eager and talented student. In 1900, she was accepted at Radcliffe College, becoming the first deaf-blind person to attend college in American history. Sullivan went with her and spent countless hours translating lecture notes and reading assignments. In 1902, a few months after her 22nd birthday, Keller began writing her autobiography, *The Story of My Life.* When she sold it for serial publication in *Ladies' Home Journal,* she decided to hire an editor, John Albert Macy, to help organize her work. Not long after Macy joined the project, he and Anne Sullivan fell in love. They were married two years later.

Keller's story gained national attention and she started receiving hundreds of letters from supporters across the country. More inspired than ever, she graduated from Radcliffe with honors and devoted herself to helping people with similar disabilities. She launched the Helen Keller Foundation in 1915 and went on to become a world-famous lecturer and author, impressing notable figures of her time, including Winston Churchill, who called her "the greatest woman of our age."

"Helen Keller is fellow to Caesar, Alexander, Napoleon, Homer, Shakespeare, and the rest of the immortals," Mark Twain once said. "She will be as famous a thousand years from now as she is today."

New Kid on the Block

Jack Kerouac turned 22 on March 12, 1944.

The Beat Generation wouldn't have been the same if a certain 22-year-old hadn't rolled into New York, got tangled up in a murder trial, and brought together some of the wildest, rowdiest creative types in the process.

Jack Kerouac's arrival at the Columbia University campus in 1943 marked his second trip to the Ivy League school. A high school football star, Kerouac had enrolled there four years earlier on a full scholarship but broke his leg and eventually dropped out. He joined the Merchant Marine, then the Navy, then was discharged on psychiatric grounds, and had returned to Manhattan's Upper West Side to settle down with his girlfriend, Edie Parker.

Not long after his 22nd birthday, Kerouac met a young poet named Lucien Carr. Kerouac appreciated Carr's incessant revelry. They got drunk together often, sang loudly in the streets, and inhaled Benzedrine—an amphetamine that Kerouac was addicted to his whole life.

Carr was plugged into the artistic fringes of Columbia and started introducing Kerouac to his cronies. Kerouac once recalled meeting the soon-to-be-famous poet Allen Ginsberg when he was a freshman. "The door opened and in walks this spindly Jewish kid with horn-rimmed glasses and tremendous ears sticking out, seventeen years old, burning black eyes, and a strangely deep voice," he said.

Kerouac fit in well with this growing mixture of Bohemians, intellectuals, poets, and philosophers. He also struck up a close friendship with the group's elder statesman, 30-year-old William S. Burroughs, a Harvard graduate from an affluent St. Louis family who had an extraordinary drug habit.

Just as the Beat Generation was being born, however, tragedy struck. In August 1944, Carr stabbed to death a male acquaintance who was making sexual advances. After the incident, Carr tracked down Kerouac at Burroughs's apartment and begged him to hide the murder weapon. Kerouac consented and buried the knife.

The slaying made headlines. Carr was charged with second-degree murder, and after police finished their investigation, Kerouac and Burroughs were arrested as accomplices to the crime. Burroughs's parents posted his bond, but Kerouac didn't have enough money and went to jail. While in his cell, he decided to marry his girlfriend as a way, many claim, to raise bond money from both his and her parents.

Carr made a plea deal for a shorter sentence, and though Kerouac was eventually cleared of the crime, he kept his word and married Edie Parker. The union didn't stick. Within two months, the 22-year-old Kerouac left his wife and moved in with Ginsberg. With the murder ordeal still haunting them, Kerouac and Burroughs wrote alternating chapters of an unpublished roman à clef titled *And the Hippos Were Boiled in Their Tanks.*

While living with Ginsberg, Kerouac watched the Beat ideals —a new literature, a new sexuality—develop around him and he had a vision that he would become the "divine scribe" of this new generation. In 1946, he met Neal Cassady and launched a series of cross-country road trips that would spawn the acclaimed novel *On the Road.*

"Bad Films Gave Me the Courage."

Stanley Kubrick turned 22 on July 26, 1950.

"Perhaps it sounds ridiculous, but the best thing that young filmmakers should do is to get hold of a camera and some film and make a movie of any kind at all," Stanley Kubrick once said. He should know; that's exactly what he did when he was 22.

A below-average student, Kubrick did only two things well at his high school in the Bronx: He played chess and took dazzling photographs. In fact, by the time he graduated (barely), he was already a published photographer. On his way to school the day after President Franklin Roosevelt died, he snapped a picture of a sad newspaper vendor. Kubrick took the image to *Look* magazine, which paid him $25 for it on the spot.

Bad grades kept him out of college, so to make ends meet, Kubrick played chess for quarters at Washington Square Park in Manhattan. Playing up to twelve hours a day, he usually made enough to pay his bills. He also kept selling random photos to *Look* and eventually landed a regular freelance job there.

By the time he was 22, Kubrick was married, living in Greenwich Village, and itching to do greater things. He went to the movies often with Alex Singer, one of his best friends from high school. Singer was working as an office boy at Time, Inc., producers of *The March of Time* series, and a major distributor of cinema newsreels. During one of their frequent talks about films, Singer told Kubrick he should make a short documentary and he would help him sell it as a newsreel. The idea hit Kubrick like lightning.

"I was aware that I didn't know anything about making films, but I believed I couldn't make them any worse than the majority of films I was seeing," he once said. "Bad films gave me the courage to try making a movie."

Kubrick had recently sold a series of photos to *Look* about a day in the life of boxer Walter Cartier, an up-and-coming middleweight. With Cartier's permission, Kubrick returned to shoot another day-in-the-life project, this time with a motion-picture camera.

The result was the 16-minute black-and-white film *Day of the Fight,* which Kubrick shot, directed, and edited himself. He paid for it with savings he accrued from the chess tables. The shooting cost him only about $900, but Kubrick decided he wanted to add an original music score, which wound up costing him another $3,000.

While he was finishing it, *The March of Time* went out of production and newsreels were being replaced by television news. With no other contacts in the film industry, Kubrick made a cold call to RKO. The company saw the film, liked it, and bought it for $4,000, netting Kubrick only $100 in profit.

But when the 22-year-old saw his movie for the first time on the big screen at New York's Paramount Theater, he was overcome with joy. He had found his life's calling. He quit his job as a photographer the next day and devoted himself to making movies.

After making two more newsreels and a pair of feature films, Kubrick made *Paths of Glory* in 1957, which cemented his place in Hollywood history. He went on to make several classic films, including *Spartacus, Dr. Strangelove, 2001: A Space Odyssey,** and *Full Metal Jacket.*

*See David Bowie, page 14.

Crop of the Cream

Estée Lauder turned 22 on July 1, 1930.

A chemist named John Schotz spent long hours over a gas stove in 1930, trying to brew up a new kind of facial cream for women. He taught his 22-year-old niece how to concoct creams, as well, and the lesson proved to be the turning point in the young woman's life.

Estée Lauder fell in love with the process of making lotions and creams. In her uncle's makeshift laboratory, she said, she spent "every possible spare moment [cooking] up little pots of cream for faces. I always felt most alive when I was dabbling in the practice cream."

In the spring of 1932, she also discovered she had a passion for sales. She peddled her and her uncle's creams on beaches and in spas around New York, and even went to beauty salons and pitched the product to women having their hair done.

"I have never worked a day in my life without selling," she once said. "If I believe in something, I sell it, and I sell it hard." The 22-year-old succeeded. She created a word-of-mouth buzz about her creams and over the next several years developed a wide range of beauty products in her kitchen. She also started approaching executives at top Manhattan department stores to give her a counter to sell her beauty products.

In 1946, she and her husband founded the Estée Lauder Company and in 1948 established their first counter space at Saks Fifth Avenue. By the 1960s, she had turned her tiny home business, which had started as kitchen experiments with creams, into a multimillion-dollar cosmetics empire.

"Cheesy" Beginnings

Lucy Lawless turned 22 on March 29, 1990.

The woman known the world over as Xena, Warrior Princess, got her first big break acting in a "really bad, cheesy commercial" when she was 22.

"I did this sort of embarrassing commercial for travel," Lucy Lawless once recalled. "I wore a bathing suit, and I am not a bathing suit girl. . . . But they seemed to like me and I got another one after that."

Born in Auckland, New Zealand, Lawless got married at 20 and won the Mrs. New Zealand competition at 21. She was eager to start an acting career but found success only in the advertising circuit. However, the commercials finally paved the way for her first television acting job.

At the end of her 22nd year, Lawless won a role on the comedy sketch show *Funny Business,* where she showed off the natural comic timing that would later add charm to her best-known character, the Warrior Princess.

Lawless worked several other jobs until landing the title-character role in *Xena* in 1995, a show that became a phenomenal success around the globe and set records in syndication.

Internal Affair

Monica Lewinsky turned 22 on July 23, 1995.

Every person in this book experienced a pivotal moment at age 22. Only one person's moment, however, jolted a nation and led to the second presidential impeachment in U.S. history.

Monica Lewinsky arrived at the White House a few weeks before her 22nd birthday. The product of an affluent West Coast family and a string of elite private schools, she was eager to make an impression inside the Beltway.

One of about 1,000 unpaid interns at the White House that summer, Lewinsky was assigned to work in the office of Chief of Staff Leon Panetta. Her intense drive and cheerfulness made her a standout. Some of her colleagues remembered her as polite and sweet, others as immature and deceitful.

Within a few months, Lewinsky started annoying several staffers by constantly mentioning her interactions with President Bill Clinton. "She would come into our office . . . and tell stories," said an intern who worked with her. "It would be things like she got a message from the president, and he needed to see her as soon as possible, or the flowers she got on her desk were from the president."

By her own account, Lewinsky began a sexual relationship with Clinton in November 1995. In December, she was moved to a paid position in the Office of Legislative Affairs, where she hand-delivered letters from members of Congress to the Oval Office.

By the spring of 1996, several high-ranking White House staffers had grown concerned over Lewinsky's "obsession" with the president. In April, she was transferred to the Pentagon, a move officials later said was a result of Lewinsky's "inappropriate and immature behavior." At the Pentagon, Lewinsky met and befriended Linda Tripp, a career government worker.

While Lewinsky started her 22nd year with a short-lived affair with the president, she ended it by spilling all the details to a less-than-trustworthy friend. Throughout the summer of 1996, Tripp secretly recorded Lewinsky's sordid tales of oral sex in the Oval Office with Clinton, whom Lewinsky had by then nicknamed "the creep" and "schmucko."

Tripp gave the tapes to independent prosecutor Ken Starr, who dropped his investigation into the Whitewater scandal to focus on Clinton's apparent affair with a White House intern.

After the story broke on the online Drudge Report,* Clinton vehemently denied the allegations, saying, "I did not have sexual relations with that woman."

In 1998, Lewinsky was granted immunity from prosecution in exchange for details about the affair. Clinton, on the spot, finally admitted having an "inappropriate relationship," which sparked charges of perjury and an impeachment hearing.

After occupying headlines for two years, Monica Lewinsky moved to New York and launched a new career as a handbag designer.

*See Matt Drudge, page 33.

Birth of a Porn Queen

Linda Lovelace turned 22 on January 10, 1971.

At age 22, Linda Boreman, a sweet, free-spirited young woman from Yonkers, New York, transformed herself into Linda Lovelace and became the star of the most popular porn movie in history.

Boreman, the sheltered daughter of a New York City cop, was set to enroll in computer school and dreamed of opening her own boutique. But a serious car wreck laid her up for months and derailed her plans.

During her recuperation in Fort Lauderdale, Florida, she met and fell in love with Chuck Traynor, a bar owner and small-time criminal with links to the Mob. Boreman didn't know much about sex at the time, but Traynor said he would teach her.

He was an amateur hypnotist and often put her under to increase her sexual appetite. He was also an occasional pimp and pressured her to turn tricks. Years later, Lovelace said Traynor forced her into prostitution at gunpoint, and that she was often beaten and threatened. Several people who knew her at the time, however, claimed she truly enjoyed sex with strangers and was a more than willing partner.

Either way, when Traynor's bar went bust in 1971, the couple moved to New York to try to break into the burgeoning porn business. At age 22, Boreman took on a new name, Linda Lovelace, got silicone breast injections, and started making "loops"—five-minute sex films that were shown at peep shows. Lovelace made dozens of these, didn't make much money, but met several top players in the industry.

She got her big break at a cocktail party for swingers. She and Traynor met Gerard Damiano, a leading director of soft-core porn films who worked for the Colombo crime family. Damiano wanted to cast Lovelace in his newest project, tentatively titled *The Doctor Makes a Housecall,* which he envisioned as a feature-length porn film with numerous characters and an actual plot—a novelty at the time.

He not only convinced Lovelace to sign on (and paid Traynor $1,250 for her appearance), but also got the Mob to give him $25,000 so he could finance a six-day shoot in Miami. At that time, most porn movies were shot in one day in apartments near Times Square.

The script contained plenty of corny lines, silly songs and sound effects, and unusual sex scenarios. Lovelace starred as a sexually frustrated woman who goes to a doctor for help. The woman learns a new sexual technique called "deep throating" and performs it on several men until she finds the right one to marry.

Lovelace's costar Herbert Streicher, aka Harry Reems—a struggling actor who had done Wheaties commercials and some Off-Broadway work—later said, "I think all of us there knew we were present at a significant moment in sexual history."

He was right. The sixty-one-minute movie was released as *Deep Throat* in the summer of 1972 and was an unbelievable success. Screened at several mainstream cinemas across the country, it grossed $100 million in its first year, making it the most profitable film of all time. The movie single-handedly launched the "porn chic" era—the period in the 1970s when it was fashionable to see and be seen at skin flicks. Among the film's biggest fans were Frank Sinatra, Vice President Spiro Agnew, Warren Beatty, Truman Capote, Shirley MacLaine, and Bob Woodward, whose top-secret tipster* during the Watergate scandal was nicknamed after the movie.

Lovelace rode on the film's phenomenal success for a few years but soon retired from the business, divorced Traynor, and launched a lifelong crusade against pornography. "I wouldn't do any of that again," she once said. "Even if I could get $50 million." She wrote a book about her experiences, *Ordeal,* and even testified before the Meese Commission on Pornography in 1986.

*See Diane Sawyer, page 132.

A Vision in Prison

Malcolm X turned 22 on May 19, 1947.

Malcolm X once said, "I'd put prison second to college as the best place for a man to go if he needs to do some thinking. If he's motivated, in prison he can change his life."

At age 22, Malcolm Little of Omaha, Nebraska, took the first step toward becoming Malcolm X, the leader of the black power movement and minister in the Nation of Islam. He discovered a new world behind bars, and he used his time there to reinvent himself, and his release as a springboard to greater things.

The son of a Baptist preacher, Malcolm grew up listening to his father urge blacks to take control of their lives. The Ku Klux Klan repeatedly threatened his family, and the Littles relocated several times before moving to Lansing, Michigan.

Malcolm's father continued to preach to the black community, despite pressure from white supremacy groups. When Malcolm was 6, his father's body was found mangled beside train tracks, and it was generally believed he was slain by the Black Legion, a Klan-like group. His mother suffered a nervous breakdown, from which she never recovered.

Malcolm moved to Boston to live with his sister. He dropped out of school after eighth grade, got addicted to cocaine, and became known as "Detroit Red," a small-time criminal. In 1946, he was sentenced to eight years on burglary and firearms charges.

He spent his first year in prison fighting with guards, smuggling in drugs, and lashing out at other prisoners. But an elder inmate, John "Bimbi" Bembry, saw great intelligence in the young troublemaker and encouraged him to develop his mind instead of wasting his life. The advice had a strong effect on Malcolm, who sought out the prison library and started reading voraciously.

Several months after his 22nd birthday, Malcolm X received a mysterious letter from his brother Reginald that read: "Malcolm, don't eat anymore pork, and don't smoke anymore cigarettes. I'll show you how to get out of prison. . . ."

The young inmate thought his brother had concocted some psychological ruse to play on the guards, so he obeyed. Malcolm's sudden self-restraint was indeed noticed by guards and inmates alike. He continued the abstinence act for several months and he liked the feeling of power it gave him. But, after he was transferred to the Norfolk Prison Colony in Concord, Massachusetts, in the spring of 1948, he learned that his brother's advice was not a trick.

All of Malcolm's siblings had joined the Nation of Islam,* a militant black organization that supported the idea of a separate black nation within the United States. His brother urged him to join the movement and study the works of its leader, Elijah Muhammad. Thirsty for knowledge, eager to expand his intellect and give his life meaning, Malcolm dived into the philosophy. "My homemade education gave me, with every additional book that I read, a little bit more sensitivity to the deafness, dumbness and blindness that was afflicting the black race in America," he later wrote.

Malcolm X read everything his family sent him and he wrote hundreds of letters to high-ranking members of the Nation of Islam, including Muhammad. "I still marvel at how swiftly my previous life's thinking pattern slid away from me. It is as though someone else I knew of had lived by hustling and crime," he said. "I would be startled to catch myself thinking in a remote way of my earlier self as another person."

When he was released from prison four years later, he changed his name to Malcolm X to indicate the unknown name of his African ancestors, which was removed by white slave owners. Malcolm X became a forceful civil rights leader, and parted with the Nation of Islam in 1963 to form his own group. In 1964 he made a pilgrimage to Mecca, where he announced his conversion to orthodox Islam and his new vision that blacks and whites could achieve a peaceful brotherhood. He was assassinated in New York City in 1965 by three men claiming to be Black Muslims, but his legacy and influence in the black power movement endures to this day.

*See Muhammad Ali, page 2.

High Country

Cheech Marin turned 22 on July 13, 1968.

Cheech Marin owes much of his fame to a topless bar in Vancouver.

When he dropped out of California State University at Northridge just eight credits shy of an English degree, Richard "Cheech" Marin realized he was a prime candidate for service in the Vietnam War. The Los Angeles native and son of an LAPD cop decided to move to Canada, where he could dodge the draft and smoke lots of marijuana, or, as he put it, "pursue pottery."

He arrived shortly after his 22nd birthday and ventured into a topless bar owned by Tommy Chong, a professional musician and songwriter who had played with Bobby Taylor and the Vancouvers, a Motown band.

Cheech and Chong became friends and launched a musical/performance art troupe called City Works. The group put on a variety of shows at Chong's bar, from psychedelic rock performances to improv comedy.

"It was great, you could call it modern-day burlesque," Marin once recalled. Soon, however, audiences demanded more comedy and less music. Surrounded by potheads and hippies, Cheech and Chong started aping the youth drug culture and poking fun at their own Latino stereotypes.

When City Works finally collapsed, the duo started performing as "Cheech and Chong" and attracted larger and larger audiences. By the end of the 1960s, they were headlining major comedy clubs in Toronto, New York, Chicago, and Los Angeles, where they eventually relocated.

Because their act typically attracted young people, Cheech and Chong also started opening for and touring with rock bands, including the Rolling Stones and the Allman Brothers Band. In the early 1970s, the pair started recording comedy albums, including *Big Bambu* and *Los Cochinos,* which made them national celebrities

The duo made six feature films, including the 1978 hit *Up in Smoke* and 1983's *Still Smokin,* before breaking up in the mid-1980s to pursue their own careers. Marin's lesser-known claim to fame contradicts his clueless, pothead persona: He was the first Celebrity *Jeopardy* Champion.

Mystical Dream

Bob Marley turned 22 on February 6, 1967.

The man whose name is synonymous with reggae adopted a new religion at 22 and reinvented his look, his sound, and his message.

The son of a white Jamaican-born plantation overseer and a black teenager, Bob Marley grew up in rural north Jamaica. When his father abandoned the family when Marley was 6, Marley's mother relocated to Trench Town, a slum in Kingston named for the sewer that ran through it. He listened to rhythm and blues music from a radio station in New Orleans and with his pals Neville "Bunny" Livingston and Peter McIntosh dreamed of playing music.

When they were teens, the trio formed a band called the Wailers and played ska—a combination of R&B and mento, a local folk sound, that was gaining popularity thanks to the island's biggest celebrity, Jimmy Cliff. The Wailers recorded dozens of singles and enjoyed some success on local stations.

In 1963, Marley's mother moved to Delaware with her new husband and pleaded with her son to one day move to the United States with her. Marley finally consented to give America a shot in 1966—but not before marrying his longtime girlfriend, Rita Anderson. He told her he would return and got on a plane the day after their wedding.

Marley worked several odd jobs in Delaware: He was a lab assistant at DuPont, a security guard, and an assembly-line worker at Chrysler. But he quickly grew to dislike the pace of life in the United States. "Everything was too fast, too noisy, too rush-rush," he once said.

An introvert, Marley made no new friends and spent all of his spare time plucking a guitar and writing lyrics. With the money he was stashing away, he dreamed of returning to Kingston and starting his own record label.

Sometime around his 22nd birthday, Marley had a dream that stuck with him the rest of his life. A man in khakis approached him and said he was sent by Marley's dead father to deliver a ring with an unusual black jewel. He handed it to him and said, "This is all I have to give you."

When he woke, he told his mother about it. Astounded, she retrieved the exact ring he had described. It had belonged to his father. Marley put it on but quickly removed it, saying it made him extremely uncomfortable.

While he was in America, his wife, Rita, adopted Rastafarianism after Haile Selassie I, the king of Ethiopia and the living god of the Rastas, made an official visit to Jamaica. This Judeo-Christian faith maintains that Ethiopia is the true Zion, and that Western society is the modern version of Babylon, corrupt and oppressive. Rastas believe marijuana is sacred for its spiritual effects, and stress nonconformity and nonviolence.

When 22-year-old Bob Marley finally returned to Jamaica, he told his wife about the dream he had in Delaware and she urged him to see a Rasta elder about it.

Marley approached Mortimo Planno, who interpreted the vision as a test from God to see if Marley was more interested in material wealth or spiritual fulfillment. Marley offered several interpretations of the dream over the years, but in any case, he adopted Rastafarianism, grew dreadlocks, returned to his band, and started writing songs that reflected his new beliefs.

Bob Marley and the Wailers recorded for several years before releasing their breakout album *Catch a Fire* in 1973. Two years later, their song "No Woman, No Cry" became a hit around the world and made Marley one of the most famous Jamaicans in history.

"There Is No Anything!"

Steve Martin turned 22 on August 14, 1967.

"I was either going to become a professor of philosophy or a comedian," Steve Martin once said. "Then I realized the only logical thing was comedy because you don't have to justify it." That realization hit him when he was 22.

Everything Martin did while growing up in Los Angeles set the tone for his career in comedy. As a teenager, he worked part-time at Disneyland and the Knotts Berry Farm theme park, where he developed juggling, banjo, and magic acts. But when he enrolled in California State University at Long Beach, the young performer decided to devote himself to philosophy. "College totally changed my life. It changed what I believe and what I think about everything," he once said. "I majored in philosophy and started studying logic. They were talking about cause and effect, and you start to realize, 'Hey, there is no cause and effect! There is no logic! There is no anything!'"

Three years into his major, Martin dropped out, transferred to the theater department at UCLA, and signed up for several creative writing courses. He also delivered his first stand-up act at the Prison of Socrates, a nightclub on Balboa Island. "It was Hoot Night, and I got up and just threw everything in to try and get fifteen minutes," Martin recalled. "So I had my magic, and I read poetry and played the banjo, and I juggled. It's exactly what I'm doing now."

At a time when most comedians were aping the harsh, cynical style of Lenny Bruce, Martin's zany sense of humor and childlike absurdist punch lines were a welcome relief to many audiences. He quickly found a manager and signed a contract.

The real turning point in his career occurred toward the end of his 22nd year. Martin's girlfriend was a dancer on *The Smothers Brothers Comedy Hour,* and she put him in touch with the TV show's head writer, Mason Williams. "I had written a stack of things in college, in creative writing class . . . and she showed him my stuff," he said. Williams decided to take a chance on the unknown writer. "He paid me out of his own pocket at first."

Soon, Martin's talents proved great enough that he was offered a full-time job. He also started writing for, and occasionally performing on, other popular shows, including *The Glen Campbell Goodtime Hour* and *The Sonny and Cher Comedy Hour.* In 1969, Martin shared an Emmy for outstanding comedy writing for his work on *The Smothers Brothers.*

Martin later got his big break as a performer with a series of appearances on *The Tonight Show* with Johnny Carson, which in turn led to work on *Saturday Night Live.* He went on to star in dozens of box-office hits and also wrote a best-selling novella, *Shopgirl,* and starred in the movie version.

Family History

Margaret Mitchell turned 22 on November 8, 1922.

The author of one of the most famous novels in American history got her first taste of professional writing at age 22, an experience that altered the course of her life.

Margaret Mitchell grew up in Atlanta listening to endless Civil War tales from her family, many of whom experienced the war firsthand and struggled through the Reconstruction. She loved the passion and drama of the stories—even if she didn't always get the whole story. She didn't know until she was 10, for example, that the Confederates actually lost the war.

But her love of family and the South caught up with her while she was attending Smith College in Northampton, Massachusetts. Mitchell dropped out of the school just after her final exams and after her mother's death and returned to Atlanta, where her mother had died amid the great influenza pandemic of 1918—a horrifying experience that Mitchell later conjured up to describe the death of Scarlett O'Hara's mother in *Gone With the Wind.*

After her mother's funeral, Mitchell decided to stay in Atlanta. At age 22, she thought she'd tap into her storytelling heritage and looked for work as a reporter. She landed a job at the *Atlanta Journal,* where she proved her journalistic merits and was soon assigned a weekly column for the paper's Sunday edition. Her love of writing blossomed at the newspaper.

A few years later she married John Marsh, the man who encouraged her to write a book while she was laid up in bed with a broken ankle. Mitchell started *Gone With the Wind* in 1926 and finished it ten years later.

Red Velvet

Marilyn Monroe turned 22 on June 1, 1948.

Before she became the most famous sex symbol in the world, Marilyn Monroe got into a minor car accident on Sunset Boulevard when she was 22. It was the least of her troubles during a year of staggering setbacks, but the incident turned out to be the single biggest turning point in her life.

In early 1949, Monroe was out of work, depressed, and unable to pay the rent. If anyone was used to misery, however, it was she. Born Norma Jean Baker, she grew up in foster homes and orphanages, was almost smothered to death at age 2, was reportedly raped at age 8, and started working full-time in a orphanage kitchen at age 9. She later worked in an aircraft munitions factory, where she met and married her first husband, a man she called Daddy, at age 16.

She dreamed of being an actress and started auditioning for parts all over Hollywood. She had more luck modeling, however, and at 19 was featured on the cover of *Family Circle*. It was then that she transformed herself from brunette Norma Jean Baker to platinum blonde Marilyn Monroe.

The flashes of national exposure she gained from magazine covers landed her bit parts in several forgettable movies. She thought she was on her way, but she was dropped from major studios as quickly as she was signed. She lost her most promising contract, with Columbia Pictures, a few months after her 22nd birthday.

Having tasted success, Monroe's sudden turn of fortune was harder to bear. She divorced her husband, enrolled in acting classes, and tried to find modeling work. Soon, she couldn't make the rent, and by the spring of 1949, she couldn't afford gas for her car.

But her fender bender on Sunset Boulevard changed her life. An

Associated Press photographer, Tom Kelley, happened to witness the accident and afterward introduced himself. He told Monroe he shot pictures of nude women for pinup calendars on the side and asked her if she was interested in posing. "I asked her to do the calendar. It wasn't much of a job, only fifty dollars," he later remembered. "She said no. But about a week later she changed her mind. She said she could use the dough."

Monroe was literally penniless: She arrived at Kelley's studio unable to pay the cab driver. The photographer had to pick up the fare. But the two-hour photo shoot, just four days before her 23rd birthday, turned Monroe's life around and produced one of the most iconic images of the twentieth century.

During what became known as the "Red Velvet" shoot, Kelley had Monroe pose nude on a lush, crimson drape. Ten stunning photographs were published in pinup calendars that hung in gas stations, Army barracks, and locker rooms across the country. Monroe later joked about the famous photo session, saying, "It's not true I had nothing on, I had the radio on."

Within six months, Hollywood agent Johnny Hyde offered his services to Monroe. She accepted and he instantly got her a part in *The Asphalt Jungle* in 1950, which in the same year led to her breakout role in *All About Eve.*

Monroe's reputation as a worldwide sex symbol was complete when Hugh Hefner bought the rights to one of the Red Velvet photos, called "Golden Dream," and used it as the centerfold in his inaugural issue of *Playboy* in 1953.

Monroe went on to star in several blockbuster movies. Not long before her mysterious death in 1962, she said, "Being a sex symbol is a heavy load to carry, especially when one is tired, hurt and bewildered."

Reefer Madness

Bill Murray turned 22 on September 21, 1972.

Bill Murray had a major change of vision in his early 20s, and he has an enormous stash of pot to thank for it.

"When I started out, originally I wanted to be a doctor. I was at Regis College in Denver and I was very seriously pre-med," Murray once said. "I wanted to be some kind of emergency surgeon* who would be down in the Caribbean going from island to island in paradise where I would be the only doctor for a hundred miles, and everyone would really need me in these life-or-death situations. But something happened, and I had to drop out, and so then I took up acting."

What happened was a customs agent at Chicago's O'Hare Airport caught him trying to smuggle nine pounds of marijuana. The year was 1970, and Murray was a 20-year-old pre-med student starting his second year of college. He was arrested on drug-possession charges, but a judge released him on probation because he was a first-time offender. He decided to drop out of college before his criminal record got him kicked out.

The incident fit a pattern of deviance in Murray's life: He was an unruly child and was kicked off his Little League team and out of his Boy Scout troop. Despite his chronic waywardness, Murray exhibited tremendous drive and ambition throughout his youth. To avoid getting what he thought was a second-rate education at a public high school in Wilmette, Illinois, Murray worked with his older brother Brian as a golf caddy to pay for his own tuition at a private school. (Those long days on the course later provided a gold mine of material for *Caddyshack,* which Brian wrote and Bill starred in). He did well in private school and easily gained admission to the pre-med program at Regis.

But by the winter of 1970, Murray's dreams of an exotic medical career in the Caribbean were scuttled. With nothing else to do, he started a string of odd jobs. He made pizzas. He hauled concrete. He spent two years loafing, much like the main character in *The Razor's Edge,* a novel that made a strong impression on him and that he later turned into a movie.

Not long after his 22nd birthday, however, Murray made a decision that changed his life. He tried his luck with stand-up comedy in Chicago, where his brother Brian was making a name for himself on the club circuit. Murray tested his talents at several small clubs, and in 1973 after two auditions, he joined Brian in the cast of the famous Second City** comedy troupe.

Taken under the wing of John Belushi, Murray began to hone his act. His razor-sharp wit and incredible intensity made him a standout. He always seemed on the brink of exploding—someone heckled him and he shocked (and delighted) the audience when he verbally destroyed the man and his wife.

At age 22, Murray had discovered a perfect forum for allowing his temper to run free, and his peers appreciated the sense of danger and recklessness he brought to the stage. Belushi and Murray left the troupe to join *The National Lampoon Radio Hour* in New York.

Murray hit a setback, however, when producer Lorne Michaels drew together the best of the hip new comedians for an edgy NBC ensemble show to be called *Saturday Night Live.* Many of Bill's peers—John Belushi, Dan Aykroyd, Gilda Radner—were hired, but Bill was left behind and forced to watch as the show's popularity skyrocketed.

Murray's prospects in comedy weren't solidified until Chevy Chase announced he was quitting *SNL* after its inaugural season. Murray was tapped as his replacement and spent the next three years in the cast. He and his brother made *Caddyshack* in 1980, around the time he would have finished his medical degree if he hadn't been busted with marijuana.

Murray went on to make several hit movies, including *Stripes,*

Ghostbusters, Rushmore, and *Lost in Translation,* for which he won a Golden Globe for best actor.

*See Giorgio Armani, page 8.
**See Mike Nichols, page 108, and John Belushi, page 13.

Road Rage

Ralph Nader turned 22 on February 27, 1956.

The three-time presidential candidate who once said, "Turn on to politics, or politics will turn on you," got turned on himself at age 22 when he witnessed a gruesome car accident.

Ralph Nader was hitchhiking home from a semester at Harvard Law School when he saw a low-speed accident in which a young girl sitting in the backseat was decapitated by a poorly attached glove compartment that broke apart and struck her on impact. He was horrified and outraged by the fatal defect in the car. That was the day Ralph Nader says he became a consumer advocate.

He wrote numerous angry letters to automotive safety organizations, as well as a seething essay on the car industry for one of his courses. He became a constant voice in the op-ed section of Harvard's student newspaper. Even after he graduated, Nader published an article in *The Nation* about the tragic accident he had witnessed and the auto industry he argued was responsible.

Though the event marked the beginning of his lifelong crusade to protect American consumers, Nader let the issue rest—that is, until 1964, when then-Assistant Secretary of Labor Daniel Patrick Moynihan asked him to help prepare a federal report on traffic safety. Nader tackled the study with diligence and enthusiasm, and his work was later published in the book *Unsafe at Any Speed,* which exposed the auto industry's gross negligence in major safety issues.

The book propelled Nader to the frontline of consumer advocacy and his numerous followers became known as "Nader's Raiders." He unsuccessfully ran for president in 1996, 2000, and 2004.

Brother-in-Law Enforcement

Eliot Ness turned 22 on April 19, 1925.

The man who took down legendary gangster Al Capone was working a tedious job for a credit lender when his brother-in-law suggested he enter law enforcement.

After graduating from the University of Chicago with a degree in business and law, Eliot Ness got a position at the Retail Credit Company, based in Atlanta. His main task was to perform background checks on people applying for loans, and he was assigned the Chicago territory. The work proved to be extremely dull, and Ness, an avid reader since childhood, filled his free time reading Sherlock Holmes stories and Agatha Christie mysteries.

His sister's husband, Alexander Jamie, was an agent in the Justice Department. He often took Ness to the firing range and taught him how to shoot. When he saw Ness unhappy in his job, he encouraged him to quit and become a federal agent. Ness took the advice and at age 22 enrolled in night classes in criminology.

As Ness worked toward his master's degree, Jamie helped get him a job at the Treasury Department. Ness was assigned to the 300-person Prohibition Bureau, which prosecuted criminals in the bootlegging business. Ness was thrilled by his career change. "Unquestionably, it was going to be highly dangerous," Ness once said. "Yet I felt it was quite natural to jump at the task. After all, if you don't like action and excitement, you don't go into police work. And, what the hell, I figured, nobody lives forever!"

In 1929, Ness led a team of agents solely dedicated to taking down Al Capone. They called themselves "the Untouchables," and they made headlines every time they disrupted some facet of Capone's underworld empire. For three years, they tried to corner him. Finally, in 1931, Capone was arrested and sent to prison on tax evasion charges.

Partnering Up

Mike Nichols turned 22 on November 6, 1953.

One of the few artists to win every major entertainment award —Oscar, Emmy, Tony, and Grammy—Mike Nichols got his start in show business when he met a witty young woman named Elaine May.

Born Michael Igor Peschkowsky in Berlin, he immigrated with his family to the United States when he was 8 years old to escape the Nazi regime. He decided to pursue comedy while attending the University of Chicago. After graduation, he helped found the Compass Players, an improv group that was later renamed the Second City* and which produced several top-notch comedy actors, including Ed Asner, Alan Alda, and Jerry Stiller.

While working with the Compass Players, Nichols met fellow member Elaine May when he was 22 years old. The pair had a magnetic stage chemistry and began performing skits together. Audiences responded so well to their shows, they launched their own act apart from the troupe.

From 1953 to 1961, Nichols and May were one of the most successful comedy acts in the country. They released an album of their work in 1960, which won a Grammy Award. After that, Nichols turned to the stage and directed his first Broadway show, *Barefoot in the Park,* starring a then-unknown Robert Redford,** in 1963.

Nichols went on to direct numerous critically acclaimed films, including *The Graduate, The Birdcage, Primary Colors,* and *Closer.*

*See John Belushi, page 13, and Bill Murray, page 103.
**See Robert Redford, page 117.

Need Not Apply

Sandra Day O'Connor turned 22 on March 26, 1952.

The first female U.S. Supreme Court justice in history owes her trailblazing career to workplace sexism she experienced at age 22.

Growing up on a cattle ranch in Arizona, Sandra Day O'Connor intended to follow her parents and become a rancher. She studied economics at Stanford with that purpose in mind, but when her family got tangled in a legal dispute over their land, she decided law might be a better pursuit. She not only finished Stanford Law School in just two years, instead of three, but also ranked third in her class—first was future Supreme Court Chief Justice William Rehnquist.

But when she entered the job market, O'Connor learned that her achievements meant little in the male-dominated legal world of the early 1950s. Plenty of law firms in California interviewed her, but none wanted to hire her. In fact, the only job offer she got was as a legal secretary. Appalled by the lack of opportunities for women in the private sector, O'Connor decided at age 22 to go into the public arena. She quickly found a position as the deputy county attorney of San Mateo, California, where she worked for about two years. "That job influenced the balance of my life," O'Connor once recalled, "because it demonstrated how much I did enjoy public service."

After living a few years in Germany, O'Connor returned to Arizona, where she was named assistant attorney general in 1965. She became a state senator and then was appointed to Arizona's Court of Appeals. In 1981, she became the first woman on the U.S. Supreme Court after being nominated by Ronald Reagan.*

*See Jerry Falwell, page 35, and Ronald Reagan, page 115.

Let's Call the Whole Thing Off

Jacqueline Kennedy Onassis turned 22 on July 28, 1951.

The *New York Herald* ran a wedding announcement on January 21, 1952, that read: "Jacqueline Bouvier to be June Bride of John Husted Jr." That forecast fell apart, however, when the 22-year-old bride-to-be met a young congressman named John F. Kennedy two months later at a dinner party in Washington.

Born to a wealthy family in Southampton, New York, Jacqueline Bouvier spent her teenage years at Miss Porter's School, Vassar College, and the Sorbonne in Paris. When she graduated from George Washington University with a degree in art, she had so many ambitions she didn't know what career to pursue.

"I always wanted to be some kind of writer or newspaper reporter," Bouvier once said. "But after college . . . I did other things." Among them, she became a photographer and developed a talent for snapping candid portraits of politicians, which earned her a job at the *Washington Times-Herald.* The newspaper nicknamed her "the Inquiring Camera Girl" and sent her to cover numerous functions and parties inside the Beltway. She had a penchant for making her subjects relax by asking them random off-the-wall questions. The newspaper often ran those amusing interviews in the captions next to her photos.

Bouvier met and fell in love with stockbroker John Husted in 1951. In December, she accepted his marriage proposal. The well-known debutante and her fiancé made headlines in society pages throughout the winter, but in March, Bouvier was assigned to photograph Kennedy, a Massachusetts representative who was running for the Senate.

Kennedy was known as the most eligible bachelor in Washington and when he asked Bouvier out on a date, she accepted. Bouvier called off her engagement to pursue this new romance that was born. "It was a very spasmodic courtship, conducted mainly at long distance with a great clanking of coins in dozens of phone booths," she said.

Kennedy won the Senate election and in September 1953, he and Bouvier were married in Newport, Rhode Island, sparking the beginning of a family dynasty that would become known as Camelot.

In Vogue

Dorothy Parker turned 22 on August 22, 1915.

One of the sharpest wits of the twentieth century started off her 22nd year in miserable monotony: She played piano at a dance school, pounding out the same tunes over and over again. By the time she was 23, however, she had published her first poem and was a staff writer at one of the most popular magazines in the country.

Dorothy Parker, née Rothschild, grew up in New York City, writing poetry and short stories as a child. She started sending out her work at the end of her teens but had no luck getting published. To pay the bills, she took a job at a dance studio but languished in boredom. Finally, at 22, she sold her poem "Any Porch" to *Vanity Fair*.

The exposure helped her get an interview at the magazine's sister publication, *Vogue,* where she was hired to write captions for the high-end women's glossy. Not very interested in haute couture, Parker gained a reputation for her humorous and offbeat captions of women posing in the latest fashions. One of her notable creations read: "There was a little girl who had a little curl, right in the middle of her forehead. When she was good she was very very good, and when she was bad she wore this divine nightdress of rose-colored mousseline de soie, trimmed with frothy Valenciennes lace."

After several months, an editor at *Vanity Fair* noticed Parker's humorous and highly stylized writing and offered her a job as the drama critic at the magazine. The 22-year-old grabbed the opportunity, which marked a significant turning point in her life.

During her tenure at *Vanity Fair,* she not only met her future husband, Edwin Pond Parker, but also a range of authors, editors, and playwrights, who would hold regular "Round Table" meetings at the Algonquin Hotel. Parker became known as one of the sharpest wits in the group and went on to publish dozens of acclaimed short story and poetry collections, including *Laments for the Living* and *Death and Taxes.*

A lifelong drinker, Parker once suggested that the epithet on her tombstone should read: "This is on me."

Westward Motion

Brad Pitt turned 22 on December 18, 1985.

Silver screen heartthrob Brad Pitt dropped out of college just a month shy of graduating to try his luck in Hollywood—an adventurous move that led to his first acting job in, ironically, the TV sitcom *Head of the Class.*

At age 22, Pitt had had enough of college, even though he was a mere two credits away from an advertising degree at the University of Missouri in Columbia and an extremely popular man on campus. He dropped out, packed everything into his used Datsun, and drove to California.* "In my head, I was done with college," he later said. "I was on to the next thing."

The next thing turned out to be a string of bizarre, and sometimes humiliating, odd jobs. He chauffeured strippers in a limo; he delivered refrigerators; and, in ostensibly his first acting job, he dressed up as a chicken and handed out flyers at the grand opening of the Mexican restaurant El Pollo Loco in North Hollywood. In any case, he was able to put food on the table. "Those jobs kept me in Cap'n Crunch and peanut butter and jelly," he said.

He was also able to pay for acting lessons and started what would be a six-year tutelage under acting coach Roy London. He finally got his break at the end of his 22nd year in a bit part on *Head of the Class.* That led to a bit part on *Growing Pains,* which led to semi-regular roles on *Dallas* and the soap *Another World.*

Pitt didn't achieve real fame, however, until his appearance in the 1991 film *Thelma and Louise,*** which paved the way for his leading-man status in dozens of blockbuster movies.

*See Matt Drudge, page 33, and Woody Guthrie, page 53.
**See Susan Sarandon, page 130.

Radio Days

Ronald Reagan turned 22 on February 6, 1933.

The president known as "The Great Communicator" was given an opportunity as a radio announcer at age 22 that proved pivotal to the course of his life.

Ronald Reagan studied economics and sociology at Eureka College in Eureka, Illinois, and when he graduated in 1932 found himself in the same predicament as millions of others during the Great Depression: unemployed. He had long dreamed of becoming a sports announcer, so the eternal optimist packed his bags for the big city. "I decided to hitchhike to Chicago to hunt for a job as a radio announcer. I met rejection everywhere I went," he once said. "I was practically laughed out the door, usually without even an interview."

Reagan returned home in frustration and decided to try his luck at smaller radio stations around the Midwest. He was finally given a chance at WOC in Davenport, Iowa, when during an interview the station manager asked Reagan to announce an imaginary football game—and to make him believe he was listening to the real thing.

Reagan, a college football star known as "Dutch," excitedly grabbed the mike and improvised: "Here we are in the fourth quarter with Western State University leading Eureka College six to nothing. Long blue shadows are settling over the field and a chill wind is blowing in through the end of the stadium."

The manager never stopped him. Reagan delivered a twenty-minute play-by-play account of an entire fictional fourth quarter—complete with a heart-stopping final play. He was offered a job on the spot. Unfortunately, however, the position was temporary and Reagan was soon laid off as a result of budget cuts.

Distraught, he spent the holidays jobless, reading about how the country was sinking deeper into the Depression. He remembered that winter as particularly cold and for two months was paralyzed by the bleakness of his future. All that changed a few days after his 22nd birthday.

"I've often wondered at how lives are shaped by what seem like small and inconsequential events," he said. "In February, I got a telephone call that changed everything." An announcer had quit at WOC, and the manager offered Reagan a full-time job. Reeling with excitement, he accepted a $100-a-week position. Announcing real sports events proved harder than imaginary ones. Reagan struggled through his first few weeks. "I was not an immediate success, to put it mildly. . . . I stumbled over my words and had a delivery as wooden as a prairie oak," he said. "But I began practicing my delivery to get the right rhythm and cadence and give my words more emotion."

The station eventually merged with WHO in Des Moines, and Reagan relocated there as chief sports announcer. He developed a mesmerizing storytelling style, announcing games from a wire ticker as though he were seeing them firsthand. Once, when the ticker machine failed in the ninth inning of a heated Chicago Cubs game, Reagan faked the game for six minutes—with a batter hitting foul balls—until the wire was back up.

"At twenty-two I'd achieved my dream: I was a sports announcer," Reagan said. "If I had stopped there, I believe I would have been happy the rest of my life." But he didn't stop there. He became a local celebrity and in 1937 traveled to Hollywood for a screen test. He ended up appearing in more than fifty films, before launching his monumental career in politics.

Aimless Artist

Robert Redford turned 22 on August 18, 1959.

Bored, depressed, drunk, and adrift—that was Robert Redford when he was 19. But by 22, the aimless youth had found a woman, found a calling, and found his big break.

Born in Los Angeles at the end of the Great Depression, Redford grew up to be a poor student and a bad influence on his peers. He was good at baseball, however, and managed to win an athletic scholarship to the University of Colorado—a boon for his parents, who couldn't afford to send him to college.

He moved to Boulder, started pitching for the team, but quickly returned to his lazy ways. He started skipping classes, skipping baseball practice, and hitting the bottle hard. "I was headed for the edge," Redford admitted.

He was finally booted off the team and kicked out of college. He returned to California only to face another misfortune: the death of his mother. He decided he couldn't stay in Los Angeles, and with nothing else to do, he worked in an oil field to save up money for a ticket to Europe. Redford had taken a few art classes in Boulder and decided he would become a painter.

"I left Los Angeles and I never really went back," he said. "I have no horror of L.A., but there's a sadness when I'm there. It was home."

He took a steamship to France in 1955 with the goal of studying art in Paris.* When he landed, however, wanderlust hit him and he started traveling instead, painting wherever he could along the way. He spent eighteen months crisscrossing the continent, living in poverty, but for the first time thinking about the meaning of his life. "I was living with a bunch of bohemians, highly politicized, and I'd be challenged by students about my country and I didn't know what they were talking about," he said.

After he returned to California, his new motivation in life quickly subsided to his old boredom. He was fired from several jobs, including grocery bagger and apprentice carpenter. But in 1958, he met Lola Jean Van Wagenen, a woman who helped him find his direction again.

The couple married about six months after they met, and Lola encouraged Redford to give up drinking and take up painting again. They packed up for New York, where Redford enrolled in the Pratt Institute in Brooklyn. Living in a tiny apartment on the West Side, which he called "a real hellhole," Redford paid the bills by working nights as a janitor and a mailroom clerk. "I used to go to the skating rink in Rockefeller Plaza just to get a sense of peace—the way some people might go to church," he said.

He realized he had no real talent for painting and was too impatient to improve his skills. But he enjoyed a class he took in theatrical set design, and he befriended the professor, who happened to moonlight as a Broadway stage manager.

A few months after his 22nd birthday, Redford got the break that would change his life. The art professor got him a small part in the Broadway show *Tall Story*. Redford enjoyed acting so much, he enrolled in the American Academy of Dramatic Arts.

By the early 1960s, he was landing roles in numerous plays and television shows, including *Barefoot in the Park* and *The Twilight Zone*.** He became an international star with *Butch Cassidy and the Sundance Kid* in 1969 and went on to star in, produce, and direct many more successful films.

*See Christie Brinkley, page 17.
**See Mike Nichols, page 108, and Rod Serling, page 134.

Government Job

Condoleezza Rice turned 22 on November 14, 1976.

The first black woman to serve as U.S. secretary of state, Condoleezza Rice got her first taste of Beltway politics at age 22.

Condoleezza Rice, whose first name is adapted from the Italian *con dolcezza,* meaning "with sweetness," grew up in Birmingham, Alabama, reading voraciously and aspiring to be a classical pianist.* Rice graduated early from high school, and after the family moved to Colorado, she enrolled as a music major at the University of Denver when she was only 15 years old.

However, after taking a course in international politics—taught, coincidentally, by the father of future secretary of state Madeleine Albright—Rice had a change of vision. She abandoned her piano major and switched to political science. The next stop after her graduation at 19 was the University of Notre Dame, where she got her master's degree in 1975.

A Democrat during her teens, Rice reevaluated her political stance after graduation and registered as a Republican. Though the move signaled a shift in opinion, it did not prevent her from pursuing her first political job in Washington under a Democratic president, Jimmy Carter.

In 1977, at age 22, Rice landed an internship in the Bureau of Educational and Cultural Affairs, which was in a section of the government she would one day lead: the State Department. The experience played a major role in her growing interest in international affairs—specifically with Soviet and Eastern European countries—as well as her determination to work in politics.

Rice went back to academia first, however, receiving her Ph.D. in international studies in Denver and then becoming an award-winning professor at Stanford University. In 1986, she returned to Washington as special assistant to the director of the Joint Chiefs of Staff—a post that led to a string of ever-higher-ranking appointments from both Presidents Bush.

See Ansel Adams, page 1, and Jamie Foxx, page 44.

Comic Timing

Chris Rock turned 22 on February 7, 1987.

Though he started doing stand-up comedy in his teens, Chris Rock got his break in the business after being spotted by comedy king Eddie Murphy.

Growing up in Bedford-Stuyvesant, Brooklyn, Rock discovered his talent for stand-up early and began hitting open-mike nights in high school. After impressing the right people, he was given a chance to perform at New York's Comic Strip Live when he was 18—but he didn't know that one of his heroes would happen to be sitting in the audience that night.

Eddie Murphy enjoyed Rock's act so much that he introduced himself to the young comedian. The connection proved pivotal for Rock. A few years later, Murphy offered him a small role in one of his movies. Although Rock's performance at age 22 as "Playboy Mansion valet" in *Beverly Hills Cop II* wasn't exactly the breakout role of a lifetime, he did establish a friendship with Murphy that led to bigger things.

Two years later, Rock joined the cast of *Saturday Night Live,* where his brash, crude, and often outrageous sense of humor not only earned him national fame, but also paved the way for numerous HBO specials and starring roles in Hollywood.

Philadelphia Story

Norman Rockwell turned 22 on February 3, 1916.

A few weeks after his 22nd birthday, the unknown artist Norman Rockwell packed up three of his latest illustrations and took a train from New York to Philadelphia, where he had an appointment with the art editor of the *Saturday Evening Post.* Not only would the trip mark the turning point in Rockwell's life, but it would also spark the incredibly prolific career of one of the twentieth century's most popular artists.

"I paint life as I would like it to be," Rockwell once said. "I unconsciously decided that if it wasn't an ideal world, it should be."

He always knew what he wanted to paint and he always knew growing up that he wanted to devote his life to art. But after some early successes—he sold several illustrations for Christmas cards at age 16—Rockwell joined the Navy during World War I and returned to New York with few job prospects.

He moved to New Rochelle, New York, just north of the city, and shared a studio with cartoonist Clyde Forsythe. As Rockwell honed his craft, Forsythe encouraged him to submit his work to the *Saturday Evening Post.** Rockwell, who had always considered the widely read *Post* the "greatest show window in America," decided to take his roommate's advice.

Equipped with his three best illustrations, the 22-year-old traveled to Philadelphia and met with art director Walter Dower, whom he hoped would buy at least one of his paintings. Rockwell was made to wait in a lobby while Dower looked over the work. When he finally appeared again, the man told Rockwell that the magazine would not only buy all three illustrations, but commission three more.

Rockwell went home elated. On May 20, 1916, his first illustration, *Boy with Baby Carriage,* appeared on the cover and his reputation as a portrayer of hometown America was established. The artist went on to paint 321 covers for the *Post* over the next 47 years, creating a collection of paintings that have been among the best-selling and most-beloved in American history.

*See Theodor "Dr. Seuss" Geisel, page 49.

"Teacher of Tricks"

Karl Rove turned 22 on December 25, 1972.

Just about everything Karl Rove has done in his professional life is but a repetition—though perhaps on a grander scale—of a feat he pulled off at age 22.

In 1973, the young man forever obsessed with Machiavelli concentrated all of his talents and energies on a single election. In the process, he was accused of dirty campaigning, espionage, and stealing votes. Yet, not only did he achieve his objective, but he also escaped all allegations unscathed and was even rewarded for them. In short, he became Karl Rove.

While attending the University of Utah, the lifelong Republican became obsessed with political campaigning. He was so hell-bent on acquiring political power that he dropped out after two years to pursue his ambitions full-time.

After his 22nd birthday, Rove spotted his opportunity: the national chairmanship of the College Republicans. He decided to launch a full-scale assault for the election against popular incumbents Bob Edgeworth and Terry Dolan.

After driving around the South stumping for the race, Rove arrived at the convention in June 1973 at the Lake of the Ozarks, in Missouri. He went around identifying the delegates who had come to vote for his opponent—and then tried to disqualify them because they lacked proper credentials. (During his national tour, Rove had circulated a new College Republicans constitution and handpicked his own delegates, whom he credentialed under the laws of that constitution.)

Exactly twice the number of expected delegates had arrived to vote: One group for Edgeworth, one group for Rove. The result: Two constitutions produced two sets of delegates, which produced two candidates who declared themselves the winner. Edgeworth and Rove appealed to the Republican National Committee, which was led by George H. W. Bush. The RNC launched an investigation in the summer of 1973 to decide who had won the election.

During the investigation, however, Rove was caught in a moment of supreme hubris. He was touring the country giving talks to College Republicans and boasting about his campaign tricks, or "pranks," as he called them. In Lexington, Kentucky, Rove talked about rummaging through garbage to dig up dirt on opponents.

He also recounted a stunt he'd pulled in 1970 on Illinois state senator Alan Dixon, who was planning an open-bar social for a reelection campaign. Rove stole reams of Dixon's stationery and then circulated flyers all around Chicago with the words, "Free beer, free food, girls and a good time for nothing" for anyone who showed up at Dixon's headquarters. The event, attended by high-society campaign contributors, became swamped with homeless people.

Of course, it was the summer of Watergate, and after regaling the crowd with his nefarious tales, Rove urged the College Republicans to remember the primary rule of campaign subterfuge: Don't get caught.

Ironically, Rove's speech was recorded and a tape of it fell into the hands of Edgeworth's running mate, Terry Dolan. Dolan seized the opportunity to ruin Rove and leaked the tape to the *Washington Post.* The newspaper published the story next to its ongoing Watergate coverage, with the headline: "GOP Probes Official as Teacher of Tricks."

Nixon and the Republican Party were in the midst of a major damage-control campaign, and more proof of party improprieties, however minor, did not help their cause. Bush decided to end the College Republicans skirmish once and for all. Rove had been caught boasting about his tricks; Edgeworth's people had leaked it to the press. Bush picked his man. He declared Rove chairman and excoriated Edgeworth for the leak. To Bush, the person who aired the party's dirty laundry was far worse than the person who dirtied it in the first place.

Rove, at age 22, assumed control of the College Republicans, moved into his Washington office, and was even further rewarded for his political caginess: Bush made him one of his special assistants.

The most pivotal year in Rove's life drew to an end with perhaps its most pivotal moment. The day before Thanksgiving 1973, Bush asked Rove to pick up his eldest son, who was flying in from Harvard.

Years later, Rove recalled meeting George W. Bush and the instant love he had for him. He had "huge amounts of charisma, swagger, cowboy boots, flight jacket, wonderful smile, just charisma. He was exuding more charisma than any one individual should be allowed to have."

After running his own public affairs firm for two decades, Rove went on to work on all four presidential campaigns of the Bush family and earned a reputation as a kingmaker.

Life's a Drag

RuPaul turned 22 on November 17, 1982.

After performing on a variety show on public-access television, one of the most famous drag queens in the world got his first taste of show business at age 22 when he was asked to join an up-and-coming punk band in Atlanta.

Growing up in San Diego, RuPaul Charles was an effeminate boy and remembers being frequently called a sissy from as early as age 4. By 15, he knew he was gay and moved in with his sister in Atlanta, where he felt more empowered to be himself and dress as feminine as he liked. "We are all born into the world naked. The rest of it is just drag," he once said.

In 1981, he put together his first cross-dressing music act, RuPaul and the U-Hauls, and managed to get a slot performing on a public-access program called *The American Music Show*. He fell in love with performing: "We were a smash hit!" he recalled.

At 22, RuPaul flooded Atlanta with posters reading "RuPaul Is Red Hot" and gained enough attention to attract several offers to team up with other bands. But he decided to join a new wave/punk band called Wee Wee Pole, a choice that paid off.

Throughout 1982, Wee Wee Pole featuring RuPaul and the U-Hauls attracted a large following in Atlanta. RuPaul became a local celebrity on the drag-club circuit. After the group disbanded in 1983, the young transvestite was forced to seek more mundane employment, but the experience had changed the course of his life.

In 1987, he moved to New York and started landing bit parts in television and movies, including *Saturday Night Live,* Spike Lee's *Crooklyn,* and *The Brady Bunch Movie.* He got his own talk show on VH1 in 1996.

Birth of Holden Caulfield

J. D. Salinger turned 22 on January 1, 1941.

By the time he was 22, aspiring author J. D. Salinger had a growing collection of rejection letters from literary magazines all over the country. But a few months before he was shipped off to fight in World War II, he finally sold a story to the *New Yorker*—and in it first appeared Holden Caulfield, the disillusioned teenager who would make Salinger one of the most renowned writers of the twentieth century.

A native New Yorker, Salinger graduated from Valley Forge Military Academy in Pennsylvania, where he'd acted in several plays. He enrolled at New York University in 1936 but soon dropped out to work as an entertainer aboard a Caribbean cruise ship. That venture was equally short-lived, and Salinger next decided to pursue a writing career. He signed up for a short-story-writing course at Columbia University in 1939.

Though he worked diligently, by 22 he had published only one story—in his professor's literary magazine. After repeated rejection from major publications, he was thrilled when the *New Yorker* offered to purchase "Slight Rebellion off Madison" in 1941. The magazine chose not to publish the story, however, until five years later, just after World War II.

Encouraged by the sale, Salinger continued to develop his principal characters in the story: Caulfield and a girl he tries to seduce, Sally Hayes. His work was sidelined, though, when he was drafted as an infantryman in the Army. Salinger went on to participate in some of the bloodiest battles of the war, including the D-day invasion at Normandy and the Battle of the Bulge, experiences that affected him deeply and put him in a psychiatric hospital for several months.

When he returned to the United States in 1947, he dived back into writing and found numerous outlets for his work. He sold several short stories to the *Saturday Evening Post, Collier's,* and *Esquire.* Then, in 1951, he finished his novel about Holden Caulfield and published it as *The Catcher in the Rye,* a highly acclaimed novel that secured his place in American literary history.

Cattle Call

Susan Sarandon turned 22 on October 4, 1968.

Even though Susan Sarandon graduated with a bachelor's degree in drama, she had no real intentions of becoming an actress. But at age 22, she accompanied her actor husband to an audition, and that changed everything.

While studying a range of subjects at the Catholic University of America in Washington, D.C., including philosophy and military strategy, Susan Tomalin fell for a graduate student in one of her drama classes, Chris Sarandon. The two soon moved in together, and because the religious college frowned on such arrangements, they got married.

To pay the bills, she worked as a secretary, cleaned apartments, and took up modeling: Her first job was posing for a brochure for the now-infamous Watergate Hotel. Along the way, she grew to admire her husband's commitment to acting. "He played a huge part in my decision to become an actress," she once said.

The biggest part he played, in fact, was dragging her to a cattle-call audition in New York for the controversial movie *Joe.* Before the audition, Chris Sarandon's agent asked Susan to read the opposite part as "a warm body for him to play against." The agent liked Susan's performance so much, he insisted she audition as well. Chris was rejected; Susan, with no formal training, landed a major role.

The movie, starring Peter Boyle, was released in 1970, and Sarandon's portrayal of a disaffected teen who disappears into a seedy underworld launched her acting career. In 1970, she won a regular role on the daytime soap opera *A World Apart* and in 1975 landed the part that made her famous in the cult classic *The Rocky Horror Picture Show.*

She divorced Chris Sarandon in 1979 and began dating actor Tim Robbins in 1988. Her other credits include *Bull Durham,*

*Thelma and Louise,** and *Dead Man Walking,* for which she won an Academy Award.

*See Brad Pitt, page 114.

"Weather Maiden"

Diane Sawyer turned 22 on December 22, 1967.

During her first semester in law school, Diane Sawyer had a change of heart. The 22-year-old dropped out, visited a local television station, and applied for a reporting job. She landed a spot as a weathercaster, a sudden career shift that forever altered the course of her life.

Born in Glasgow, Kentucky, Sawyer and her sister competed in numerous beauty pageants growing up. When she was 16, the future anchorwoman won both Kentucky's Junior Miss and America's Junior Miss pageants, which brought $11,000 in prize money. Sawyer used it to pay tuition at Wellesley College, where she received an English degree in 1967.

That fall, she enrolled at the Louis D. Brandeis School of Law at the University of Louisville, where she intended to follow the career path of her father, a county judge. But after one semester and weeks after her 22nd birthday, Sawyer pulled up stakes and decided to go into news journalism. And landing a job as "Weather Maiden" at WLKY-TV was the best start she could find.

"I did the weather for a while . . . most memorably, in the days of the cone bras," Sawyer once recalled. "You go back and you look at my old weathercasts, and that's all you can see is like these blinking headlights. It was so awful."

She did news reports on the side and impressed her manager so much that she was taken off weather and made a full-time reporter within a year—a position she held for four years.

In 1970, she was hired to work in Nixon's White House under press secretary Ron Ziegler. Many people thought she was Deep Throat,* the unidentified informant in the Watergate scandal, though that rumor eventually proved to be false. She returned to broadcast journalism in 1978 at CBS News and went on to co-anchor the *CBS Morning News* and ABC's *Good Morning America.* She married film director Mike Nichols** in 1988.

*See Linda Lovelace, page 89.
**See Mike Nichols, page 108.

Dramatic Twist

Rod Serling turned 22 on December 25, 1946.

Creator of *The Twilight Zone* and a legend in the golden era of television, Rod Serling didn't know what to study when he returned wounded from World War II, so he majored in physical education. But several weeks after his 22nd birthday, he switched to literature and started writing plays and acting—a choice that changed his life.

The day after he graduated high school in Binghamton, New York, Serling enlisted to be an Army paratrooper. The small, wiry teen took up boxing during basic training and won 17 out of 18 bouts. He saw combat in the Pacific, was wounded, and was later awarded the Purple Heart and Bronze Star. Serling suffered from war-related flashbacks and insomnia throughout his life.

Discharged in 1946, he enrolled in Antioch College in Ohio, where he not only eventually majored in literature, but also started writing, directing, and acting in school plays and local radio productions. Serling fell in love with drama. But during an internship at a radio station, the manager told him he wasn't cut out for radio; he didn't have the voice for it.

Serling, whose narrations of *The Twilight Zone* would become iconic, ignored the criticism and started submitting his radio plays in competitions. At the end of his 22nd year, he hit it big. His script about a prizefighter slowly dying of leukemia won a national contest. Although the Emmy-winning teleplay *Requiem for a Heavyweight** wasn't produced until 1956, Serling used the prize to secure his television writing career.

After writing several plays, he created *The Twilight Zone* in 1959. While the show became famous for its eerie story lines and O'Henry-style surprise endings, Serling used the series to address controversial issues—racism, sexism, and Cold War paranoia—for the first time in television history.

*See Sean Connery, page 28.

Rock Bottom Birthday

Richard Simmons turned 22 on July 12, 1970.

Richard Simmons battled obesity throughout his youth. In college, he began a series of drastic and harmful measures to lose weight, culminating at his 22nd birthday party—arguably the lowest point in his life.

Food was the center of his life as early as he could remember. Born and raised in New Orleans, the future exercise guru grew up eating deep-fried Southern cuisine and developed a passion for unhealthy foods. "Even as a baby, I could recognize a package of bacon at twenty feet. The strips of bacon looked so weak, so flimsy, so sad, until they hit the frying pan," he once said. "Then they began swimming and dancing, lacing up at the sides and turning golden brown." By the time he graduated high school, he stood five feet eight and weighed well over 200 pounds.

An aspiring painter, Simmons won a spot in a foreign exchange program and went to study art in Florence, Italy. He poured more passion into eating, however, than painting. His growing girth even got him his first chance in show business.

A casting director for filmmaker Federico Fellini spotted Simmons and asked him to be an extra in *Satyricon.* He said he wanted Simmons because he was fat. Taking the remark in stride, Simmons was thrilled and ended up appearing in several crowd scenes.

The work led to other acting offers, and while studying art, Simmons made commercials on the side, mostly based on his girth: He played a dancing meatball in one commercial and a chubby Peter Pan who couldn't fit through a window in another.

Enjoying the attention he was getting for his figure, Simmons didn't worry about his health until he found an anonymous note left for him on his car: "Richard—You're very funny, but fat people die young. Please don't die."

The plea affected him deeply. He stepped on the scale for the first time in years. He weighed 268 pounds. Ashamed, he decided to starve himself. He dropped 112 pounds in about three months. The period of fasting wore on his body, however, and he collapsed outside a church. A doctor told him he had to start eating again; Simmons obeyed and put back on the pounds he'd lost.

A year later, with art degree in hand, Simmons moved to New York and got a job waiting tables. Still obsessed with his size, he met a woman who was bulimic and who encouraged him to purge his meals to lose weight. After gagging himself once, Simmons decided it wasn't for him—until his 22nd birthday party, when his friends took him out for a Chinese feast. "Everything we ordered was fried and sauced, and covered with peanuts or oil. I ate and ate and ate, to the point that I was ashamed," he recalled. "So, I excused myself and I went to the bathroom and locked the door."

He returned with an empty stomach and tears pouring down his face. He later said he never felt more ashamed in his life. Even so, the incident led to four more months of bulimia. He finally saw a doctor, who gave him some harsh feedback. He told Simmons the only way to lose weight and stay healthy was to eat smart and exercise. Simmons vowed never to purge his meals again. It was the turning point in his life.

In 1973, Simmons moved to Los Angeles and, frustrated by the lack of exercise facilities for obese people, started his own exercise club in Beverly Hills. The soon-to-be-renowned "Slimmons" studio encouraged overweight people to dance their way back to health. Simmons's vivacity and sense of humor reached hundreds of people, to the point that he was featured on a segment of the TV show *Real People,* which launched his path to fame.

The Artist's Way

B. F. Skinner turned 22 on March 20, 1926.

If he hadn't first failed as a novelist and poet, B. F. Skinner never would have become the world-renowned psychologist and pioneer of behaviorism.

"I did not direct my life. I didn't design it, I never made decisions," Skinner once said. "Things always came up and made them for me. That's what life is."

He may not have designed his life, but he certainly made a fateful proposition with himself at age 22. While getting his English degree at Hamilton College in New York, Skinner had the opportunity to lunch with Robert Frost. The famous poet asked to see some of Skinner's work and after reading a few of his poems urged him to continue writing.

Skinner was thrilled by the encouragement. But he decided to give himself only one year as a writer; if he hadn't found any success by then, he would quit. In the summer of 1926, he moved to New York's Greenwich Village, where he lived a bohemian life and intended to write about his experiences. The experiment was a failure. He realized he had few experiences worth serious artistic exploration and no strong viewpoints to express. He wrote almost nothing.

He stuck to his proposition, however, and at the end of the year, just after his 23rd birthday, he enrolled in Harvard to study psychology—a subject he'd read about with tremendous interest while living his artist's life.

Skinner went on to become a major critic of psychoanalysis and a leading proponent of behaviorism, a theory that all human and animal behavior is based on responses to external stimuli, not repressed memories. He also became famous for the "Skinner box"—a device he invented in which he "taught" mice to behave differently by altering their stimuli.

Hype Writer

Zadie Smith turned 22 on October 27, 1997.

One of the most celebrated debut novels in the last century started getting publicity when it was only one chapter long and its author only 22 years old.

Zadie Smith once confessed that she decided to become a writer only after giving up on her childhood dream of starring in musicals.* "From the age of five to fifteen, I really wanted to be a musical movie actress. I tap-danced for ten years before I began to understand people don't make musicals anymore," she once said. "Slowly but surely the pen became mightier than the double pick-up time step with shuffle."

Mightier indeed. Smith was studying English at King's College, Cambridge, when she showed a literary agent about eighty pages of material she'd written for a novel about a lifelong relationship between wartime friends. The agent convinced numerous publishers that Smith would become the next great writer, and held an auction for the novel based on only the small amount that was written.

The hype paid off. Publisher Hamish Hamilton won the auction and reportedly paid 22-year-old Smith an advance of $450,000. Though the young writer was still finishing her bachelor's degree, she spent the next two years working on the novel that would become *White Teeth*. "I didn't think the book would take two years to write," she recalled. "But I was quite lazy. And I had moments of fear, of not being able to write anything."

By the time she finished it, *White Teeth* was one of the most anticipated novels ever written. Readers and critics quickly determined that it was worth the wait. Smith was hailed one of the best authors of her generation and frequently compared with Salman Rushdie.

She has since written two other novels, *The Autograph Man* and *On Beauty*, which both became best sellers. She has also apparently revisited her love of musicals. In 2004, she announced she was collaborating with her husband on a stage musical about author Franz Kafka.**

*See David Hasselhoff, page 54.
**See Franz Kafka, page 75.

The Acting Bug

Sissy Spacek turned 22 on December 25, 1971.

Sissy Spacek was struggling to make it as a singer when she appeared as an extra in an Andy Warhol* film. The experience changed her outlook, and by 22, she had dropped singing, begun studying acting, and made her big-screen debut.

In 1970, the bright-eyed country girl from Quitman, Texas, got a call from her cousin, actor Rip Torn, who invited her to move to New York and try her luck in show business. The high school homecoming queen left her "happy, idyllic, small-town life," changed her name to Rainbo, and launched a singing career in the coffeehouses of Greenwich Village.

Although she found some success—she recorded a flower child-type single, "Johnny, You Went Too Far This Time," and several commercial jingles—Spacek's walk-on role in Warhol's 1970 art movie *Trash* spurred her to reconsider her priorities. With Rip Torn's help, she enrolled in Lee Strasberg's Actors Studio.

The career change paid off immediately. She landed her first credited role just after her 22nd birthday, playing a young woman sold into white slavery in the highly graphic and controversial movie *Prime Cut.*

Spacek's big-screen debut was followed that year by work on the popular TV show *The Waltons,* in which she played a girl trying to marry John Boy. She even uttered one of the shows most memorable lines: "When are you going to stop being John Boy, and start being John Man?"

From there, Spacek landed two major roles that clinched her fame: a teenage murder accomplice in the eerie 1973 movie *Badlands* and the title character in the film version of Stephen King's *Carrie,* which earned Spacek her first Oscar nomination in 1976. She went on to star in numerous movies and television shows.

*See Andy Warhol, page 160.

"Duel" Purpose

Steven Spielberg turned 22 on December 18, 1969.

One of the most famous filmmakers of all time was so frustrated by his first experience directing a television show that he took time off from the business before returning at the age of 22 to direct his debut film.

Steven Spielberg made dozens of short films as a teenager and desperately wanted to attend the University of Southern California's film school but was twice rejected. He ended up at California State University, Long Beach, where he dropped out at age 21 to sign a long-term deal with Universal Pictures.

One of Spielberg's first assignments was to direct an episode of *Night Gallery,* Rod Serling's TV show about supernatural encounters.* The episode starred Joan Crawford, and although Spielberg impressed his producers, cast, and crew, he grew frustrated by his lack of creative control. He decided to quit television directing and instead focus on films.

While rummaging around the studio's mailroom, Spielberg came across a script for *Duel,* a suspense tale about a big-rig truck that terrorizes an innocent driver. He loved the screenplay so much he asked Universal to let him direct it. At age 22, he began shooting what would become one of the cult classics of the 1970s, and the movie that won Spielberg the creative license he craved.

Duel was first released as a TV movie-of-the-week but generated so much attention, Universal released it as a feature film in 1971. From there, Spielberg directed the stunning *Sugarland Express* in 1974, before making the 1975 film that for a time was the highest-grossing in history, and that cemented his place in Hollywood: *Jaws.*

*See Rod Serling, page 134.

Rode in on a Hurricane

Ringo Starr turned 22 on July 7, 1962.

After enjoying three years as the drummer of one of the most popular rock bands in Liverpool, England, Ringo Starr was tired of the rock-and-roll lifestyle, quit the band, and at age 22 planned to move to Texas to work in a factory.

Born Richard Starkey, he grew up in a working-class family and had suffered several serious illnesses as a child. He spent so much time at the hospital and so little in school, that by the age of 15 he could barely read and write.

His stepfather gave him a drum set, and Starkey fell in love with it. He joined his first band at age 17 and with his disarming sense of humor got to know many of the big names on the Liverpool music scene. His stepfather urged him to keep music as a hobby, however, and encouraged him to pursue a trade. "I started to be an engineer, but I banged me thumb on the first day. I became a drummer because it was the only thing I could do," Starr once said. "The main thing is, I didn't ever want to go back to work."

In 1959, his flair for a back beat got him a job with Rory Storm and the Hurricanes, an up-and-coming group known for their flashy stage shows. Rory Storm persuaded Starkey to change his name to something more "cowboyish"—hence Ringo Starr was born.

By 1960, the group was the most popular in Liverpool and often headlined at the famous Cavern Club. At the time, many British rock bands were flocking to the nightclub scene of Hamburg, Germany, where Rory Storm and the Hurricanes soon landed a regular spot at the Kaiserkeller.

Meanwhile, another new band from Liverpool, the Beatles, were earning their stripes at the much less prestigious club, the Ratskeller. But soon enough, John Lennon, Paul McCartney, George Harrison, Stuart Sutcliffe, and Pete Best were asked to play at the Kaiserkeller—and got second billing to Rory Storm's group.

Although the Hurricanes were paid considerably more money and had better accommodations, the two groups became friends. Ringo hit it off with all the Beatles, especially 17-year-old Harrison, and filled in for the group's notoriously moody drummer, Pete Best, when he was sick.

By 1962, Ringo Starr had grown disenchanted with the rock-and-roll routine. He decided it was time to take his stepfather's advice and learn a real trade. He concocted a plan to go to work in Houston.

At the same time, the Beatles had secured their first recording contract. Their producer, George Martin, had little confidence in the talent of Pete Best, and other band members agreed. Best was fired in August 1962. Ringo got a call a few months after his 22nd birthday, asking if he'd like to join the Beatles. He shelved his Houston plans and said yes.

Starr showed up for his first rehearsal on August 18, 1962, less than three weeks before the band was scheduled to record an album for EMI on Abbey Road in London. He later said he felt like a newcomer during those weeks, and had a hard time breaking into the tight-knit group. No one told him, for example, that John Lennon got married to Cynthia Powell on August 23. And his insecurities doubled when another drummer, Andy White, showed up for a re-recording of "Love Me Do." White was handed the drumsticks; Starr was handed a tambourine.

Later, Martin decided Starr was the superior drummer, used his version of "Love Me Do," and never questioned his talents again. By the time the album was finished, Starr recalled, he not only finally felt a part of the band, but also knew he was on the brink of something big.

"I've never really done anything to create what happened, it created itself," he said. "I didn't do anything to make it happen apart from saying, 'Yes.'"

Ringo became an essential member of the group, and many

early fans voted him as their favorite Beatle. One of his earliest contributions beyond drumming was coining the phrase "hard day's night," the genesis of a hit Beatles song, album, and movie.*

*See *Jerry Garcia*, page 45.

Family Man

Howard Stern turned 22 on January 12, 1976.

Right out of college, Howard Stern was offered his first professional radio job. But the highly obsessive 22-year-old was so worried about making money and providing for a family he didn't yet have, he declined the offer and went into advertising. If he hadn't been persuaded by his mother and girlfriend to take a chance on radio, Stern would have never become one of the most beloved— and loathed—voices on the air.

Stern graduated magna cum laude from Boston University with a major in broadcasting and film. He worked at the college radio station, where he experimented with different broadcasting styles. One of his notable efforts was his *King Schmaltz Bagel Hour,* a parody of the famous series *King Biscuit Flower Hour,* but it was canceled after its first show for being too offensive.

He also met his future wife, Alison Berns, in college. Stern had become involved in Transcendental Meditation, which he would practice religiously throughout his professional career.* He first approached Berns by asking her to appear in a movie about TM that he was making for a class. She accepted, and the pair started dating.

After graduation, Stern returned to New York, where he was born, and landed a series of interviews at radio stations in the tristate area. But as he and Alison neared marriage, Stern began to worry about providing for a family. He turned down his first offer at WRNW, a small station in Briarcliff Manor, New York, and became obsessed with pursuing a more lucrative career. "It got so bad that I even took a bullshit job in advertising," he recalled.**

In the summer of 1976, Stern took an entry-level job at Benton and Bowles in Manhattan. He hated the work. "Thankfully, my mother and Alison persuaded me to quit and get back into radio," Stern said.

The station manager at WRNW had been impressed by Stern during his interview, and even though Stern had turned down the job, the man had kept his résumé handy. When Stern quit his advertising job, he called the station and said he was available to be a disc jockey. He finally got his chance on Christmas Day, 1976, when the station was understaffed for the holidays.

Stern's first professional radio experience was a disaster. Because of an equipment failure, he was unable to turn off any of the mikes. Listeners heard everything, even when songs were playing—the sounds of Stern sliding around in his chair, grabbing albums, loading up the next record. After dozens of listeners called in to complain, the young deejay had to call the chief engineer at home and beg him to come in.

As Stern later remembered it, WRNW was "a 3,000-watt FM toilet bowl," where employees brought their own toilet paper to work and on payday rushed to cash their checks in case the station ran out of money. But it also became the place where he developed his on-air personality. "I used the place, I made a living, I wanted to make money," he said. "I hustled, I hustled, I showed my employer how good I was."

His earliest and most successful routine was to drag random station employees—sales reps, secretaries, janitors—into the broadcast room for a chat. His tasteless banter and toilet humor boosted his popularity. "He needed someone to play off of," a colleague noted.

Fired after two years for "unacceptable behavior," Stern moved to stations in Connecticut, Detroit, and Washington, D.C., slowly expanding the amount of his show devoted to talk, and reducing the amount of time actually spent playing music.

After building a loyal audience in the early 1980s, Stern's controversial *Howard Stern Show* was syndicated by Infinity Broadcasting in 1986, and later became one of the most popular radio shows of all time.

*See Andy Kaufman, page 77.
**See F. Scott Fitzgerald, page 38.

Model of Change

Sharon Stone turned 22 on March 10, 1980.

Though she had just broken into the modeling business and was commanding large fees from ad agencies across the country, Sharon Stone decided to quit being a model at age 22 and pursue the career she'd always dreamed of: acting.

In fact, her decision was so sudden, she embarked on her new pursuit immediately after a modeling gig in Paris. "I packed my bags, moved back to New York, and stood in line to be an extra in a Woody Allen movie," Stone recalled.

As a teen, Stone had scored extremely high on an IQ test (154) and enrolled in college at age 15. She graduated from Edinboro University of Pennsylvania three years later with a fine arts degree. Her family persuaded her to enter beauty pageants, and though she lost several, she met a few promoters who told her she should go to New York to model. She took the advice, moved in with her aunt in New Jersey, and four days later landed a contract with the famous Ford modeling agency. Soon she was appearing in national print and TV ads for Clairol, Revlon, Diet Coke, and Burger King.

Her work took her to Europe, where she realized she was in the wrong business. She wanted to be creative. A big fan of old movies, Stone decided to try acting. She returned to New York and landed the tiny role of "Pretty Girl on train" in Woody Allen's *Stardust Memories.* "It was only a bit part and I didn't get to speak," she said. "But I felt that I was in a real movie and heading where I had always wanted to be."

Thrilled by her big-screen debut, Stone went on a barrage of auditions. Just before her 23rd birthday she landed a speaking part in the horror movie *Deadly Blessing,* which then led to regular roles on several popular TV shows, including *Remington Steele, Magnum P. I.,* and *T. J. Hooker.*

Stone starred in several flops throughout the 1980s and didn't break into the mainstream until she was cast opposite Arnold Schwarzenegger in 1990's *Total Recall.* That movie led to a starring role in *Basic Instinct,* which made her an international sex symbol and led to many more leading roles. In 1998, she even starred in the animated feature *Antz,* alongside the man who gave her her first break, Woody Allen.

The Gambler

Tom Stoppard turned 22 on July 3, 1959.

One of Tom Stoppard's characters says, "Life is a gamble, at terrible odds—if it was a bet you wouldn't take it." But at age 22, the future world-renowned playwright took one of the biggest gambles of his life.

Stoppard left school in Bristol, England, at age 17, to work as a junior reporter for the *Western Daily Press* and later for the *Bristol Evening World.* He reported news and feature stories but also developed a fondness for writing theater reviews and got to know several actors and directors at the Old Vic Theatre in London.

With his notorious wit, love of language, and growing desire to write his own plays, Stoppard quit his job at the end of his 22nd year. He continued to freelance as a journalist to help make ends meet but focused his energies on completing his first one-act play, *The Gamblers,* and first full-length play, *A Walk on Water,* in 1960. Although Stoppard later credited the former as his first original work and the latter as a composite of several plays he admired, *A Walk on Water* was optioned almost immediately—though not produced for several years.

The favorable response to his early work encouraged Stoppard to ditch journalism and pursue playwriting. After getting several plays produced, he wrote one of his most famous works in 1967, *Rosencrantz and Guildenstern Are Dead.*

Stoppard went on to pen several highly regarded screenplays, including *Brazil, Empire of the Sun,* and *Shakespeare in Love,* for which he won the Academy Award.

Dressed to Kill

Mr. T turned 22 on May 21, 1974.

A college football star, Mr. T was recruited by the Green Bay Packers but suffered a knee injury that ended his athletic career. At 22, he reinvented himself as an upscale bouncer/bodyguard—a move that led to an unlikely acting career and worldwide fame.

Born Laurence Tureaud, the second-youngest of twelve children, he grew up in a Chicago housing project, where he learned the importance of acting tough. Showing and being shown respect were critical to Tureaud, and in 1972, he legally changed his name to Mr. T, so people would have to address him as "Mr."

He won a football scholarship to Prairie View A&M University in Texas but was kicked out after two years. When his knee injury ended his professional career, Mr. T returned to Chicago, where he styled himself as a bodyguard for the rich and famous. With his impressive build and intimidating presence, his career change proved instantly successful.

"I was a very dapper dresser," he recalled. "I shaved my head, wore derby hats, white gloves, three-piece suits, carried a cane. I never went anyplace without a fresh carnation or a rosebud in my lapel."

At 22, he started landing jobs protecting numerous celebrities, including Muhammad Ali,* Michael Jackson, Steve McQueen, and Diana Ross. He soon earned up to $3,000 a day. He once boasted that he never lost a client. His business card read, "Next to God, there is no better protector than I."

As his reputation in the entertainment world grew, Mr. T changed his look and adopted his now-famous mohawk and beard in the style of an African Mandinka warrior, after seeing pictures in *National Geographic.* He also worked as a top-notch bouncer and in 1982 took part in a TV contest called "The World's Toughest Bouncer." Sylvester Stallone spotted him on the program and cast him as his opponent, Clubber Lang, in *Rocky III,* which made Mr. T an international star and landed him a leading role on TV's *The A-Team.*

See Muhammad Ali, page 2.

Southern Exposure

Hunter S. Thompson turned 22 on July 18, 1959.

After writing two short novels when he was 22—and repeatedly failing to get them published—Hunter S. Thompson decided to leave fiction-writing behind forever. But the decision prompted him to invent his own brand of highly opinionated, first-person nonfiction known as gonzo journalism.

Growing up with alcoholic parents in Louisville, Kentucky, Thompson had a difficult childhood that included several brushes with the law. When he was arrested for robbery at age 19, the judge agreed to let him off easy if he enlisted in the Air Force. During his stint in the military, Thompson on a lark took a job as the sports reporter for the base newspaper.

He instantly fell in love with writing and forged his own colorful style. When he was discharged in 1958, he moved to New York and landed a job as a copy editor at *Time* magazine. He also started living like a beatnik, drinking heavily, and experimenting with drugs.

Unsatisfied as a copy editor, Thompson tried selling freelance articles to numerous newspapers, mostly focusing on his firsthand experiences of a near-poverty bohemian lifestyle, but found little success. He grew to dislike conventional journalism and at age 22 decided to move to Puerto Rico, where he applied to be a sports reporter at two newspapers. In one job-seeking letter, he wrote: "I have given up on American journalism. The decline of the American press has long been obvious, and my time is too valuable to waste in an effort to supply the 'man on the street' with his daily quota of clichés, gossip, and erotic type."

He was finally hired by *El Sportivo,* a small tabloid that covered bowling, and relocated to San Juan. In between sports stories, Thompson wrote two semiautobiographical novels: *Prince Jellyfish* and *The Rum Diary.* When no publisher would touch them, he considered it a sign that he wasn't destined for fiction. The failure forced him to reconsider journalism as a serious pursuit, and he started to hone the style he would become famous for in his 1966 breakout book, *Hell's Angels.*

In 1999, decades after Thompson's other gonzo journalism books, *Fear and Loathing in Las Vegas* and *Generation of Swine,* had made him a counterculture celebrity, Simon & Schuster bought one of those early efforts at fiction. *The Rum Diary* hit the shelves forty years after it was written.

"Software Is Like Sex"

Linus Torvalds turned 22 on December 28, 1991.

"Microsoft isn't evil, they just make really crappy operating systems," Linus Torvalds once said.

When he was 22, the computer science student decided to do something about it: He released the first version of his Linux operating system for free on the Internet. The move not only forever changed the computer software industry, but also marked a major turning point in his life.

Torvalds was born and raised in Helsinki, Finland, where his interest in programming started with his first two computers, a Commodore VIC-20 and a Sinclair QL. He learned how to modify their rudimentary operating systems by installing his own code. Torvalds also created his own video games, including a knockoff of Pac-Man called Cool Man.

While studying at the University of Helsinki, Torvalds made a hobby out of designing a new operating system that would be more efficient and less problem-prone than Microsoft's Windows. He based his code on the MINIX system, a popular classroom teaching tool, as well as UNIX, the classic operating system created by AT&T in the 1960s.

Around his 22nd birthday, he completed what became known as the Linux kernel, the source code of his new operating system. Though the program itself was remarkable, what made Torvalds famous was his decision a few months later to offer it free as an open-source code—allowing anyone on the planet to use it, modify it, strengthen it, and redistribute it.

"Software is like sex: It's better when it's free," he once said. "Making Linux freely available is the single best decision I've ever made." He posted the Linux kernel online, and by the end of 1992, it had become one of the most popular open-source operating systems in the world.

Although Torvalds is now an icon in the programming industry and has ranked on *Time* magazine's list of the 100 most influential people in the world, he has tried to stay out of the limelight. Of course, he still owns the Linux trademark and once declared himself the project's "benevolent dictator for life."

Birth of an Alcoholic

Bill W. turned 22 on November 26, 1917.

The man who cofounded Alcoholics Anonymous—and devoted his life to helping people fight substance abuse and addiction—had two major turning points in his life: The negative one happened when he was 22.

Bill Wilson was born in East Dorset, Vermont, ironically, behind the bar at his grandparents' hotel because a snowstorm prevented travel to a hospital. The trauma he felt at age 11 by his parents' divorce was doubled when his father moved to Canada and his mother to Boston: Bill and his sister were left behind to live with their grandparents.

When the United States entered WWI, Wilson dropped out of college to join the Army. He outperformed his peers during basic training in Plattsburgh, New York, and at 22 was commissioned as a second lieutenant. He later recalled the joy he felt as an officer awaiting deployment. "We were flattered when the first citizens took us to their homes, making us feel heroic. Here was love, applause, war," he once wrote. "I was part of life at last, and in the midst of the excitement I discovered liquor."

Wilson got married in New York, but soon after the wedding, his unit was shipped to England, where they encamped near Winchester. One time on leave, he took a trip to the city's grand cathedral cemetery, where he happened upon a tombstone that caught his attention. He even wrote down the epithet:

Here lies a Hampshire Grenadier
Who caught his death
Drinking small cold beer.
A good soldier is ne'er forgot
Whether he dieth by musket
Or by pot.

The inscription haunted him and he later called it an "ominous warning, which I failed to heed."

He returned from the war, moved in with his wife, and decided to pursue a law degree. His drinking was getting worse, and just before his 23rd birthday, he nearly flunked out. "At one of the finals I was too drunk to think or write," he said. "Though my drinking was not yet continuous, it disturbed my wife. We had long talks when I would still her forebodings by telling her that men of genius conceived their best projects when drunk."

For seventeen years, Wilson suffered from severe alcoholism. He made lots of money as a stockbroker in the 1920s and drank bootleg liquor day and night throughout the Jazz Age. He lost everything after the stock market crash and had to move in with his in-laws, where he lived unemployed for five years—and was almost never sober.

The other turning point in his life occurred in 1934, when Wilson, forty pounds underweight, was being treated in a hospital. An old school friend, who had successfully battled his own alcoholism, stopped by to offer help. Wilson accepted. The man inspired him to get his life back.

Wilson came out of the hospital determined to help others. With the idea that "only an alcoholic can help another alcoholic," he helped launch A. A. He decided that anonymity would be critical to the group's success and began introducing himself at meetings as Bill W.

After the *Saturday Evening Post* ran an article on A. A. in 1941, groups cropped up across the country. The organization is still going strong today.

Black and White

Alice Walker turned 22 on February 9, 1966.

The author famous for *The Color Purple* and dozens of other novels and essays on racism and sexism in the South published her first story after enduring a year of threats from the Ku Klux Klan for being in an interracial relationship.

Alice Walker worked as a civil rights activist and wrote poetry while attending Sarah Lawrence College in Yonkers, New York. The Georgia native served in the city's welfare department after graduation but continued to submit her poetry for publication. She was awarded a writing grant a few weeks after her 22nd birthday and thought about moving to Africa to write. In the end, she decided to go to Mississippi to support the civil rights movement—a decision that changed her life.

While going door-to-door registering voters, Walker, who's black, met and started dating Melvyn Leventhal, a white civil rights lawyer. Local white supremacists were outraged to see them together. When they wed just before Walker's 23rd birthday, they became the first interracial married couple in Mississippi history. "Part of the lure of our marriage was that it was illegal," Walker once recalled.

Leventhal tried civil rights cases while Walker taught school and continued her work as writer and activist—but throughout their time in Mississippi, they faced numerous taunts, death threats, and burning crosses. The experiences shaped Walker's perspective and became material for future works.

In 1967, she published her first work, "To Hell with Dying," a short story about the anxiety and depression she felt in college after having an abortion. The story received praise and helped launch Walker's writing career. She went on to pen several best sellers, including *Meridian* and *The Color Purple,* which won a Pulitzer Prize and was turned into an Academy Award–

winning movie* directed by Steven Spielberg and starring Oprah Winfrey.

*See Steven Spielberg, page 141, and Oprah Winfrey, page 168.

The Truman Show

Andy Warhol turned 22 on August 6, 1950.

The jacket photo of Truman Capote on his debut novel, *Other Voices, Other Rooms,* changed Andy Warhol's life.

The 22-year-old graphic artist not only fell in love with the writer, tracked him down at his New York City apartment, and begged to see him—but also created a series of paintings for Capote that launched his fine art career and, consequently, the Pop Art movement.

Warhol first saw the "Lolita-esque" image of the young Capote in 1948, while he was studying pictorial design at the Carnegie Institute of Technology (later Carnegie Mellon University) in Pittsburgh. Warhol wrote Capote numerous fan letters and stuffed the envelopes with stardust. None were answered.

After graduating in the spring of 1949, he moved to New York and shared a basement apartment in the East Village with seventeen other people. Determined to make it as a graphic designer, Warhol sent his portfolio to dozens of magazines and department stores. His unique style was noticed immediately and he landed endless freelance work as an illustrator.

Within his first year, his work was featured prominently in *Glamour, Harper's Bazaar,* the *New Yorker,* and *Vogue,* as well as in advertising and shop windows at Tiffany & Co. and Bergdorf Goodman. He also became renowned for his whimsical blotted-ink drawings of shoes in ads for I. Miller. Warhol, a lifelong foot fetishist, made so much money on the shoe ads, he bought his own apartment on the Upper East Side and had his mother move in with him.

"When I started out, art was going down the drain," Warhol once said. "The people who used to create magazine illustrations and the covers were being replaced by photographers. And when they started using photographers, I started to show my work with galleries."

But the budding artist still had Capote on his mind. He not only kept writing him, but also started creating drawings based on Capote's stories—drawings he hoped would get him his first gallery showing. "I never answer fan letters," Capote once said. "But not answering these Warhol letters didn't seem to faze him at all. I became Andy's Shirley Temple." Warhol even started calling Capote's apartment and staking out the building. He also began sending him the drawings, asking for his opinion. Capote never responded.

Finally, not long after his 22nd birthday, Warhol got up the nerve and rang the bell at Capote's Park Avenue apartment. The novelist was out, but his mother was home. When Nina Capote invited Warhol up for a visit, the young artist was elated. But he quickly ascertained that Mrs. Capote was less interested in getting to know him and more interested in having a drinking companion.

The pair strolled to the nearby Blarney Stone Bar on Third Avenue and spent the rest of the afternoon talking and drinking boilermakers. They returned to the apartment that evening, and Truman Capote came home to find his mother and Warhol drunk and talking about Warhol's problems. "He seemed one of those hopeless people that you just know *nothing's* ever going to happen to," Capote said. "Just a hopeless, born loser, the loneliest, most friendless person I'd ever seen in my life."

The encounter led to a brief phone friendship between Capote and Warhol. In the end, however, Capote's mother ended the connection as quickly as she had created it: She changed her opinion of Warhol, called him a "faggot," and told him never to contact her son again. Warhol complied and ceased calling and writing.

But by the end of his 22nd year, Warhol had completed several illustrations based on his Capote obsession. A few months later, he decided to go public and hold his first art show. In 1952, Warhol paid for space at the Hugo Gallery on East Fifty-fifth Street and launched his exhibition *Fifteen Drawings Based on the Writings of Truman Capote.*

The show was a big success but also a disappointment: Warhol had invited Capote and his mother to the show, but neither appeared.

Warhol went on to become a pioneer in the Pop Art movement, with his multicolor portraits of Marilyn Monroe* and Elvis Presley and his depictions of mundane objects, such as Campbell's soup cans and Coca-Cola bottles.

See Marilyn Monroe, page 101.

Master Promoter

Harvey Weinstein turned 22 on March 19, 1974.

During his 22nd year, Harvey Weinstein turned a fledgling concert-promotion company into the beginnings of a major film-production operation that would ultimately morph into Miramax, one of the most influential film companies of the past two decades.

Born and raised in Queens, New York, Harvey fell in love with the movies early on. He says he chose to go to the University of Buffalo in 1969 after skipping a grade in high school, because, unlike other state schools, it was in a big city that had more than one movie theater.

He got involved in the University Union Activities Board, an independent arts council that funded a variety of student activities, including film festivals and rock concerts. He was a natural at the art of promotions. He was also prone to nasty confrontations with other promoters. "There was a lot of resistance, because he wasn't popular," a former promoter at a rival student group recalled. "He would try and bully his way into concert situations."

Weinstein was determined to make waves as a concert promoter. He and classmate Horace "Corky" Burger flew to New York in 1972, tracked down music legend Stephen Stills, and persuaded him to perform in Buffalo. The show was a wild success and netted Weinstein and Burger $20,000. With the money and a redoubled passion for promotions, the pair formed their own concert company, Harvey and Corky Productions.

The business did so well that in 1973, Weinstein not only dropped out of college as a senior, but also convinced his younger brother Bob, who was a sophomore, to do the same. Harvey, Bob, and Corky went to work scheduling rock concerts, plays, and comedy shows all over Buffalo. They made so much money in a year that by the time Harvey turned 22, the company was ready to expand into the field he loved the most: film.

The company bought the Century Theatre, a dilapidated 200-seat movie and concert hall in downtown Buffalo. The three men fixed it up, installed offices, and began showing second- and third-run movies on Saturday nights. Weinstein credits his brother with the idea of showing three movies for the price of one. "He had a formula," Harvey said. "At eight o'clock, he'd show a good movie," which was then followed by lesser-known films.

The format was a success and brought in moviegoers all over the city. Soon, Harvey and Bob decided to leave concerts behind and focus solely on the film business. In 1979, they formed Miramax Films, named for their parents, Miriam and Max Weinstein. The company went on to produce a string of award-winning movies, including *Pulp Fiction, The English Patient, Shakespeare in Love,* * and *The Aviator.*

*See Tom Stoppard, page 149.

Miss Contour Meets the King

Raquel Welch turned 22 on September 5, 1962.

A part-time model, a full-time cocktail waitress, and a divorced mother of two living in Dallas, Raquel Welch realized she wasn't where she wanted to be at age 22. So, she packed her bags for Hollywood and within a year flipped her life upside down.

Three days after landing in Los Angeles, she met talent agent Patrick Curtis, who didn't take long to see Welch's potential. She had won numerous beauty pageants as a teen in San Diego, including Miss Contour, Miss Photogenic, and Miss Fairest of the Fair. Curtis not only agreed to be her manager, but soon became her second husband.

The couple formed a promotions company called Curtwell Enterprises, and their first success was getting *Life* magazine to run a photo of Welch in an extremely revealing bikini. That exposure got Welch cast as the "Billboard Girl" on the ABC variety show *Hollywood Palace.* She then got several bit parts in other shows, including *Bewitched, McHale's Navy,* and *The Virginian.*

But Welch's big break came just before she turned 23. After making the rounds at several movie studios, Curtis managed to get her an audition for a part in Elvis Presley's next movie, *Roustabout.* Though Welch was cast in an uncredited role, she made her big-screen debut and used it as a stepping-stone for more work in film.

In 1966, she starred in two movies that made her an international sex symbol, *Fantastic Voyage* and *One Million Years B. C.*

Settees and Chaise Lounges

Jack White turned 22 on July 9, 1997.

Five days after his 22nd birthday, Jack White was practicing guitar while taking a break from his upholstery work. He asked his wife, Meg, to keep a rhythm on his drum set and was amazed by the "childlike innocence" of her playing.

"We were just messing around and ended up playing David Bowie's 'Moonage Daydream,' which Meg is a fan of," White recalled.* "We thought it sounded really good, and we thought, 'Why don't we work on this?'" That first, pivotal collaboration spurred a radical change in both of their lives. They gave a public performance two months later, recorded at the end of the year, and soon built up a loyal fan base as the White Stripes.

Born John Anthony Gillis, Jack White grew up in a family of ten children in a lower-middle-class area of Detroit. He took up the guitar and drums as a teenager and played in several blues and country garage bands. At 15, he was offered an apprenticeship at an upholstery shop and threw himself into the work, tearing up furniture and making deliveries.

He later formed a two-piece band with the shop's owner, Brian Muldoon, who was 16 years older than he, and they produced their own three-track single, "The Upholsterers." White continued as an upholsterer after high school, auditioning for several bands on the side and finally landing a drumming job for the country-punk band Goober and the Peas.

In 1994, while playing at a bar in Grosse Pointe, he asked out the bartender, Megan White. The band broke up within a year, but Meg and Jack kept dating. When they got married in 1996, Jack took his wife's last name** and decided it was time to take his upholstery career to the next level. He started his own business, Third Man Upholstery, when he was 21. "I was mostly doing antique furniture, you know, people's settees and chaise lounges and

166

stuff like that," White once said. "I wasn't really business-minded, though. I never really loved the money part. I guess it started to hurt my business attitude."

Though he usually found enough work to pay the bills, White said he started getting into the "cartoonishness" of his job. He adopted two colors for his business, yellow and black, and made sure everything he owned fit the color scheme: His clothes, his tools, his van. "I also started trying to make an art form out of giving someone a bill for my services, like writing it with crayon, or with a yellow piece of paper with black marker saying 'You owe me $300,'" he said. "People would be like, 'What the hell is this?'"

His handcrafted business cards also failed to entertain clients. "Each one had an upholstery tack on it with red paint that looked like blood. My slogan was: 'Your Furniture's Not Dead,'" he said. "Most people didn't think it was funny. I was broke all the time."

But when, on Bastille Day, 1997, he first heard and fell in love with his wife's drumming, White rediscovered his desire to play music. The duo called themselves the White Stripes and adopted a similar cartoonishness in appearance as White did for his upholstery shop: This time everything was red and white.

When Jack landed them their first public show, opening for a well-known garage band, Meg wasn't convinced she had the skills yet to perform. But Jack encouraged her and coaxed her into the gig, and the pair made such an impression, they became regulars on the burgeoning garage-band scene in Detroit.

The White Stripes released several singles, which led up to their debut self-titled album in 1999. Never certain they were going to succeed financially, Jack White kept working at his upholstery business until 2000, when the White Stripes' second album, *De Stijl*, went platinum.

*See David Bowie, page 14.
**See Jim Bakker, page 11.

Anchors Aweigh

Oprah Winfrey turned 22 on January 29, 1976.

By age 21, Oprah Winfrey had achieved more success in radio and television than most broadcasting students dream of. But while her career seemed to skyrocket without end, it was her first major failure, at 22, that put her on the true path of her life.

Born in Kosciusko, Mississippi, to teenage parents, Winfrey had a difficult and often poverty-stricken childhood. After moving several times, she finally lived with her father in Nashville, Tennessee. He was a strict disciplinarian who made her read a book every week and write a report.

She launched her broadcasting career at age 17 when she was hired by WVOL radio as a newsreader, after the station manager heard her voice. She won a scholarship to Tennessee State University, where she majored in speech communications and performing arts. But she loved working in media so much that she decided to drop out and take a job in television. At age 19, she signed on at WTVF-TV as an anchor—the youngest, as well as the first black female, in the station's history.

Soon after her 22nd birthday, Winfrey made a decision that led to one of the most pivotal moments in her life. She moved to Baltimore and landed a job as coanchor of the *Six O'Clock News* at the ABC affiliate, WJZ-TV. She thought the move would expose her to a larger market and perhaps open the door to a national anchoring job. After a string of successes, however, she was poised for her first great failure.

In Nashville, Winfrey's warm, personal style made her a standout on the local news. But in Baltimore, she found herself constrained by the strict objectivity set by the network. Winfrey's discomfort in reading news without emotion or flair became clear. Network executives decided to move her out of the anchor chair. "I got taken off the six o'clock news, and was put on the early morning, like five-thirty," Winfrey once recalled. "I was called in and put on the edge of being fired . . . I was devastated. I was twenty-two and embarrassed . . . because I had never failed before."

Winfrey said it was the first time in her career that things hadn't "just happened" for her. "I was devastated because up until that point, I had sort of cruised. I really hadn't thought a lot about my life, or the direction it was taking," she said. "I just happened into television, happened into radio."

In the end, her failure at being an anchor produced the biggest opportunity of her life. Because the station managers had no other place to put her, they decided to let her cohost a morning talk show called *People Are Talking.* During her first appearance, Winfrey interviewed a Carvel ice cream man and an actor from *All My Children.* She said she realized on that first show what her destiny was. "I'll never forget it. I came off the air, thinking, 'This is what I should have been doing,'" she said. "It was like breathing to me. Like breathing. You just talk. 'Be yourself' is really what I had learned to do."

Although viewers took an instant liking to Winfrey, her station manager criticized her for being too sentimental. She ignored the advice and stayed on the show for eight years—until she moved to Chicago and started *The Oprah Winfrey Show,* the most-watched talk show in television history. Winfrey's phenomenal success helped make her the first black female billionaire in history.

End of the Circus

Ed Wood Jr. turned 22 on October 10, 1946.

The man widely considered the worst filmmaker in history launched his remarkably unsuccessful career in movies right after he quit the carnival at age 22.

Growing up in Poughkeepsie, New York, Ed Wood Jr. developed an early obsession with cinema. He often skipped school to watch movies, and when the theater threw away any publicity stills it received, Wood rooted through the trash and collected them. He also started secretly wearing women's clothes as a teenager and later explained that his budding transvestite tendencies were entirely nonsexual.

Wood was also incredibly patriotic. A few months after Pearl Harbor was attacked by the Japanese, Wood enlisted in the Marines and was sent to numerous battles in the Pacific. He claimed that while fighting in the Battle of Guadalcanal, he was secretly wearing a pink bra and panties beneath his uniform. He allegedly told a fellow soldier that he was more prepared to die than be wounded, because he didn't know how he would explain his underwear to medics.

He served two years in active combat duty. After his front teeth were knocked out in battle and his leg hit with several bullets, he was discharged with a Silver Star and Purple Heart in 1946. Wood reentered civilian life by joining a carnival, where he reportedly played many roles, including "the geek" and the "half-man-half-woman."

When the carnival made it to Hollywood, Wood quit. He tried to break into movies but landed roles only in small stage productions. The turning point in his life happened when he met actor Crawford John Thomas, who was also interested in making movies, had some money to invest, and liked the 22-year-old Wood and his ambitious ideas.

The men formed Wood-Thomas Pictures and got to work on their first film, a Western that Wood wrote called *The Streets of Laredo.* After shooting only twenty minutes of footage, thé pair ran out of money. Wood, however, remained undaunted and saw the disaster as the first stepping-stone in his filmmaking career.

Wood went on to create an amazing number of movies, considering all of them were ridiculed by critics and bombed at the box office. Two of his movies even became cult classics because of their extremely poor quality: *Glen or Glenda* and *Plan 9 from Outer Space.*

Songs in the Key of Bike

Frank Zappa turned 22 on December 21, 1962.

Musical prodigy Frank Zappa got his break in show business performing on an unlikely instrument in an unlikely venue: He played the bicycle on *The Steve Allen Show.*

Growing up in California, Zappa mastered numerous instruments in his teens and began forming bands to play his own experimental sounds, often fusing classical music with rock and roll. Though highly intelligent, he disdained school, once saying, "If you want to get laid, go to college. If you want an education, go to the library."

Instead of going to college, he started making low-budget movies. While his efforts went largely unrecognized, he did land his first professional music job by composing the scores to two forgettable B movies. He also freelanced as a graphic artist and began performing at a cocktail lounge in Los Angeles.

By 22, he was ready for a change. On a lark, he contacted the casting director at Steve Allen's popular variety show and said he'd like to teach Mr. Allen how to "blow bicycle." Amused, the man invited Zappa down to audition, enjoyed his bizarre act, and cast him on the program.

With Steve Allen looking on incredulously, Zappa "played" his bicycle with a completely straight face. He plucked the old Schwinn's spokes like a harp, beat the seat like a drum, and blew into holes on the handlebars like a flute. When the composition was over, Zappa neither laughed nor smiled but looked at Allen as if awaiting applause. The host awkwardly mumbled a joke and later told the casting director never to schedule "a gag" like that again.

For Zappa, the event marked a turning point. He decided to apply himself fully to music, in which he could merge his talents, his innovative ideas, and his notorious sense of humor. With money he made from scoring another movie, he bought a recording studio just before his 23rd birthday and named it Studio Z.

He formed several short-lived bands before finally creating the Mothers of Invention in 1966. The group's first album, *Freak Out!,* lampooned everything from hippies to the Beatles to rock journalists, whom Zappa once described as "people who can't write interviewing people who can't talk for people who can't read."

The band's follow-up albums *Absolutely Free* and *We're Only in It for the Money* were equally successful and earned Zappa a cultlike following.

Sources of Quotations

(Author names are missing only where no byline was given.)

Linda Robertson, "Building Ali," *Miami Herald,* February 29, 2004.

Steve Cady, "Clay Says He Has Adopted Islam Religion and Regards It as Way to Peace," *New York Times,* February 28, 1964.

Geoff Andrew, "An Interview with Robert Altman," *British Film Institute,* January 26, 2001.

Stephen Lemons, "Hollywood's Ultimate Outsider Is at Long Last the Big Daddy of American Cinema," *Salon,* August 15, 2000.

John Preston, "Pamela Anderson: Woman of Letters," *The Daily Telegraph,* October 27, 2003.

Glenn Gamboa, "Stardust Memories," *Newsday,* February 21, 2001.

Christine Giordano, "Christie Brinkley: Model, Mother, Activist," *Networking,* June 2003.

"Garth Brooks," *Hello!,* December 19, 2004.

Raymond Carver, preface to *On Becoming a Novelist* by John Gardner, HarperCollins, June 1983.

Johnny Cash, *Cash: The Autobiography,* HarperCollins, September 1, 1998.

"An Interview with Johnny Cash: Country Music Legend," *Academy of Achievement,* June 25, 1993.

Robert Kolker, "Will Sean 'Puffy' Combs Pay $2 Million to End His City College Nightmare?" *New York,* November 29, 1999.

John Sullivan, "Rap Producer Testifies of Fatal Stampede at City College," *New York Times,* March 24, 1998.

Simon Hattenstone, "Simon Hattenstone Talks to Robert Crumb," *The Guardian,* March 7, 2005.

Steve Burgess, "Brilliant Careers: R. Crumb," *Salon,* May 2, 2000.

Brett Sokol, "The Drudge Retort," *Miami New Times,* June 28, 2001.

Matt Drudge, *The Drudge Manifesto,* New American Library, October 2000.

Brenda Clements, "An Interview with Jerry Falwell," *Lynchburg News and Advance,* September 10, 1992.

Paul Schatzkin, *The Boy Who Invented Television,* Teamcom Books, September 2002.

Larry Flynt, *An Unseemly Man: My Life as Pornographer, Pundit and Social Outcast,* Dove Books, October 1996.

Robert Chalmers, "Larry Flynt: The Trouble with Larry," *The Independent,* February 22, 2004.

Jeff Silverman, "Harrison Ford Takes Off His Fedora—and Turns Humble," *Los Angeles Herald Examiner,* 1985.

Charles Reich and Jann Wenner, "Interview with Jerry Garcia," *Rolling Stone,* January 20, 1972.

Jane Goodall, *My Life with the Chimpanzees,* Aladdin, April 1996.

Kitty Ferguson, *Stephen Hawking: A Quest for the Theory of Everything,* Bantam, July 1992.

Larry King interview, "Stephen Hawking Discusses Quantum Physics and ALS," *CNN,* December 25, 1999.

Steven Almond, "Citizen Wayne: The Unauthorized Biography," *Miami New Times,* December 1, 1994.

Shaheem Reid, "50 Cent: Money to Burn," *Rolling Stone,* February 12, 2003.

Ifè Oshun, "Just Who Is 50 Cent?" *About.com,* January 15, 2005.

Hank Bordowitz, *Billy Joel: The Life and Times of an Angry Young Man,* Billboard Books, July 2005.

Pope John Paul II, *Gift and Mystery: On the Fiftieth Anniversary of My Priestly Ordination,* Image Books, November 1996.

Stephen Dowling, "The Rising Star of Norah Jones," *BBC News,* February 24, 2003.

Don Steinberg, "The Funniest Man Who Never Joked: An Oral History of Andy Kaufman," *GQ,* December 1999.

Helen Keller, *The Story of My Life,* Signet Classics, 100th Anniversary Edition, February 2002.

Jack Kerouac, *Vanity of Duluoz,* Penguin, June 1994.

Gene D. Phillips, editor, *Stanley Kubrick Interviews,* University Press of Mississippi, January 2001.

Dino Hazell, "Estée Lauder's Sale Skills Built Up Global Empire," *London Free Press,* April 26, 2004.

Lucy Lawless, "Open-Mic Interview at *Xena* and *Hercules* Convention," Burbank Airport Hilton, January 17, 1998.

Jeff Leen, "Lewinsky: Two Coasts, Two Lives, Many Images," *Washington Post,* January 24, 1998.

Joe Bob Briggs, "Linda's Life: A Sad Story, and Its Impact on Us All," United Press International, April 25, 2002.

Legs McNeil and Jennifer Osbourne, *The Other Hollywood: The Uncensored Oral History of the Porn Film Industry,* Regan Books, February 2005.

Malcolm X, *The Autobiography of Malcolm X: As Told to Alex Haley,* Ballantine Books, October 1987.

Mike Kempf, "Cheech Marin," *Chicano Visions,* July 2005.

Timothy White, "Bob Marley, 1945–1981: The King of Reggae Finds His Zion," *Rolling Stone,* June 25, 1981.

Stephen Lemons, "Steve Martin: The One-Time Madcap Comic Deity Has Become the Distinguished Elder Statesman of Humor," *Salon,* March 13, 2001.

Ben Fong-Torres, "Steve Martin Sings," *Rolling Stone,* February 18, 1982.

Harry Flashman, "Nobody Forgets Marilyn Monroe," *Pattaya Mail,* February 16, 2001.

Richard Johnson, "Murray Works on the Wild Side," *New York Post,* December 14, 2004.

Paul Heimel, *Eliot Ness: The Real Story,* Knox Books, February 1997.

Sandra Day O'Connor, "Supreme Court Justice Biographies," The Supreme Court Historical Society, March 2, 2000.

Doris Kearns Goodwin, *The Fitzgeralds and the Kennedys: An American Saga,* St. Martin's Griffin, November 1991.

David C. Heymann, *A Woman Named Jackie: An Intimate Biography of Jacqueline Bouvier Kennedy Onassis,"* Carol Publishing, May 1989.

Stuart Y. Silverstein, *Not Much Fun: The Lost Poems of Dorothy Parker,* Scribner, July 2001.

"An Interview with Brad Pitt," *Tiger Beat,* March 1986.

Ronald Reagan, *An American Life,* Simon & Schuster, November 1990.

Suzie Mackenzie, "American Dreamer: Robert Redford," *The Guardian,* August 14, 2004.

Laura Deni, "Robert Redford's Las Vegas Flop," *Broadway to Vegas,* November 26, 2000.

Edwin McDowell, "Norman Rockwell, Artist of Americana, Dead at Eighty-four," *New York Times,* November 10, 1978.

Nicholas Lemann, "The Controller: Karl Rove Is Working to Get George Bush Reelected, But He Has Bigger Plans," *New Yorker,* May 12, 2003.

Julian Borger, "The Brains: Who Is the Man the President Calls His 'Boy Genius'?" *The Guardian,* March 9, 2004.

Mack Bates, "Simply the Best: Susan Sarandon," *The Leader,* December 6, 1999.

Diane Sawyer, interviewed on *The Rosie O'Donnell Show,* NBC, January 21, 1999.

Richard Simmons, *Still Hungry after All These Years,* GT Publishing, 1999.

B. F. Skinner, *Particulars of My Life,* Knopf, February 1976.

Stephanie Merritt, "Zadie Smith: She's Young, Black, British—and the First Publishing Sensation of the Millennium," *The Observer,* January 16, 2000.

Bill Harry, *The Ringo Starr Encyclopedia,* Virgin Publishing, June 2004.

Paul D. Colford, *Howard Stern: King of All Media,* St. Martin's Press, July 1996.

Howard Stern, *Miss America,* Regan Books, October 1996.

Lar Gould, "Sharon Stone Interview," *CinemasOnline,* June 2004.

Nicole Pellegri, "An Interview with Mr. T," *The A-Team File Fanzine,* 1983.

Carol Rust, "Fear, Loathing, and Lots and Lots of Letters," *Houston Chronicle,* July 9, 1997.

Linus Torvalds, David Diamond, *Just for Fun: The Story of an Accidental Revolutionary,* Collins, June 2002.

Bill W., *My First Forty Years—An Autobiography,* Hazelden, May 2000.

Kim Curtis, "Alice Walker, Daughter Write of Their Multiracial Family," *Associated Press,* November 16, 2000.

Victor Bockris, *The Life and Death of Andy Warhol,* Bantam, August 1990.

Ken Auletta, "Beauty and the Beast: Harvey Weinstein Has Made Some Great Movies, and a Lot of Enemies," *New Yorker,* December 16, 2002.

Tobias de la Manzana, "Jack White: Your Furniture's Not Dead," *The Believer,* May 2003.

"Oprah Winfrey: America's Beloved Best Friend," *Academy of Achievement,* February 21, 1991.

Linda Botts, editor, "Loose Talk: The Book of Quotes from the Pages of *Rolling Stone* Magazine," Quick Fox Publishing, 1980.